JOURNEYS HOME:

An Anthology of Contemporary African Diasporic Experience

Journeys Home:
An Anthology of Contemporary African Diasporic Experience

(Poems and Personal Narratives)

Edited by
Salome C. Nnoromele
Lisa Day-Lindsey

Africa World Press, Inc.

P.O. Box 1892
Trenton, NJ 08607

P.O. Box 48
Asmara, ERITREA

Africa World Press, Inc.

P.O. Box 1892
Trenton, NJ 08607

P.O. Box 48
Asmara, ERITREA

Copyright © Salome C. Nnoromele and Lisa Day-Lindsey 2009

Cover design: Ashraful Haque
Book design: Dapo Ojo-Ade

Library of Congress Cataloging-in-Publication Data

Journeys home : an anthology of contemporary African diasporic experience (poems and personal narratives) / edited by Salome C. Nnoromele, Lisa Day-Lindsay.
    p. cm.
  Includes bibliographical references.
  ISBN 1-59221-712-5 (cloth) -- ISBN 1-59221-713-3 (pbk.)
1. American literature–African American authors. 2. African Americans–Literary collections. 3. American literature–21st century. 4. Immigrants–United States--Biography. I. Nnoromele, Salome, 1967- II. Day-Lindsay, Lisa.
  PS508.N3J68 2009
  810.8'0896073--dc22
                                    2009032112

Contents

Acknowledgements

We thank the contributors for sharing their stories with us. The joy, sadness, and struggles reflected in each work remind us cogently the meaning of home and the challenges of living in exile. We also thank the College of Arts and Sciences, The Department of English and Theatre, and the African/African-American Studies program at Eastern Kentucky University for providing the resources to make the publication of this volume possible.

Prologue

Where Is Home, Anyway?

The idea for this collection began with just that—an idea, a faint whisper that grew louder and louder until I could no longer ignore its voice or its demands. I left Nigeria in 1986, too young at the time to think about the future or the implications of leaving home. I had no expectations of my new life in a new country and frankly did not anticipate any challenges. Yes, I was young and naïve. But that was more than 21 years ago, and a lot has happened since then. I have visited home four times since leaving: the first in 1993, then 2000, then 2005, and, more recently, in 2008. On visiting home in 1993 and in subsequent years, I am always reminded of a passage in Elizabeth Inchbald's novel, *A Simple Story*. The passage reads:

> Throughout life, there cannot happen an event to arrest the reflection of a thoughtful mind more powerfully, or to leave so lasting an impression, as that of returning to a place after a few years absence, and observing an entire alteration in respect to all the persons who once formed the neighborhood—To find some, who but a few years before were left in bloom of youth and health, dead—to find children left at school, married, with children of their own—some persons who were in riches, reduced to poverty—others who were in poverty, become rich—those, once renowned for virtue, now detested for their vice—roving husbands grown constant—constant ones, become rovers—the firmest friends changed to the most implacable enemies—beauty faded. . . (221)

In 21 years, I have lost two grandmothers, two uncles, a brother, and numerous other relatives. I have missed my sisters' weddings. I have had four children. My parents have grown old without the benefit of knowing my children, except for the occasional visits and the frequent chats on the telephone. My children have very resigned and vague memories of their grandparents, and practically no relationship with them. I am always struck and perplexed by the strain in my children's voices as they try to talk and communicate with my parents over the phone: the difference in experiences, the misunderstandings that come from lack of shared values and experiences, the constant tip-toeing and forced politeness, and the soft-gloved conversations that really amount to nothing, except for the satisfaction that comes from knowing that one's parents and grandparents are still alive.

My home country has changed as well. Every day, I am yet bewildered by the growing gap of expectations existing between my sisters and me, my parents and me, my other relations and me. Of course, I have been able to work and send money home to keep alive the everlasting reputation that America is a land of opportunity where food is in abundance, money could be gotten easily, and nobody ever has to work for money. And, if one has to work, finding a good job is easy and not demanding at all. One particular holiday season, the spirit of generosity moved me to send gifts to my sisters, one of whom called me elatedly to thank me and remind of how much "enjoyment" I was having "over there." On my recent visit, my mother joyfully suggested that I send my sisters money (dollars) frequently. "They are very glad to receive money from their big sister," she said. I was tempted to ask "what money?" and to suggest that I too would love to receive money from my sisters once in a while. No kidding. All of my four sisters are college graduates and gainfully employed. At that moment, however, I did not respond to my mother's suggestion. I remained mute, trying to negotiate in my mind the differences between perception and reality, rich and poor, and the gradations in between.

I do not deny that I am "enjoying" myself in my adopted country. But, part of that enjoyment includes having to define and explain myself wherever I go, and the constant feeling of being an outsider. W.E.B. DuBois in *The Souls of Black Folks* writes, "Between me and the other world, there is ever an unasked question: unasked by some through the feelings of delicacy; by others through the difficulty of rightly framing it. All, nevertheless, flutter around it. They approach me in a half-hesitant sort of way, eye me curiously or compassionately, and then, instead of saying directly, How does it feel to be a problem? they say, I know an excellent colored man in my town" (9). The American public's approach to the issue of immigration today is no less crude as was its approach to the question of race at the end of the nineteenth and beginning of the twentieth century when DuBois wrote his essay. For the most part, the immigrant is an oddity that must be contained and defined. The questions asked are no less direct than those asked of DuBois. But, instead of being asked, however subtly, "How does it feel to be a problem?" the immigrant is barraged with seemingly benign questions:

"Where did you come from?"

"How did you find your way here, of all places in the world?"

"Do you like it here?"

"Do you plan to return?"

One can live in a town for 25 years and still be asked these questions almost every day. All one needs to do is

Prologue

to open one's mouth to utter a sentence, and then the questions begin. However friendly the interrogator may be, the questions only go to the heart of the immigrant experience—a reminder of one's "outsider" status, that one is not "home." But as I was once asked by another immigrant, "Where is home and who is home, anyway?" So whenever she meets someone new, she begins asking the questions herself. "I know the questions will inevitably come," she says, "so why not take the offensive and attack before you are attacked. After all, we all came from somewhere else."

Life in exile is intriguing and exciting and complex and challenging. The exile is constantly trying to negotiate the demands of home and abroad, while keeping one's sanity and dignity intact. The stories and poems in this collection offer a beginning discourse on rather neglected but poignant aspects of life everywhere. Africans can be found outside their homelands in every country around the world. Their experiences will make one laugh, cry, smile, and wonder at the life of the immigrant, the blend and clash of cultures, the pain and triumphs.

Salome C. Nnoromele

Introduction

Global Migration and the African Experience

Even though political pundits may give the impression that immigration is a twenty-first century phenomenon, the fact is that leaving one's place of birth to settle in another land or location has been a constant part of human history. In their book *Global Migration and the World Economy*, Timothy Hatton and Jeffrey Williamson suggest that migration has been going on for centuries throughout the world (Hatton & Williamson, 2005). Close examination of world history affirms their viewpoint and indicates that human societies are always in motion. The reasons that people move are not a big mystery. Prior to the nineteenth century, and still to a smaller extent today, millions of people were forced to leave their places of birth for distant lands, where they served as slaves, as domestic servants, or as conscripted soldiers in foreign armies. Others move today, for similar reasons as five centuries ago: to improve their lives either through education and better employment opportunities, or to settle peacefully among strangers.

What is different today is the increasing attention being paid to immigration in the news media, political arenas, and in academia. As more and more people, primarily from developing nations, migrate to seek opportunities in the industrialized nations of Western Europe and North America, questions are raised about the impact of immigration on global economy and politics. The International Organization for Migration in Geneva considers migration one of the defining issues of the twenty-first century. According to their statistics, the global stock of international migration doubled in thirty years to 175 million peoples in 2000. This rate has not slowed; in 2008, the number of peoples living outside their countries of birth stands at 192 million. If we were to place all current emigrants into one geographical space, they would make up the fifth largest nation in the world, in terms of population—indeed a defining issue of our times.

First Phase of the African Diaspora:
Presently, much of the attention to immigration focuses on the countries that receive new residents. Too often, when countries of origin are mentioned in the media and in academic studies, the information is reductive at best. The African continent, a major origin of emigrants to the western hemisphere, has seen its share of both forced and unforced emigration. Although relatively complex, scholars place the trend of African external emigration into four historical phases: before the 1400s, 1400-1900, 1900-1950, and 1950-present.

Prior to the fifteenth century, Africans were traversing the Atlantic Ocean and the Sahara desert to trade as well as to settle in new lands. However, the period between the fifteenth through the end of the nineteenth century witnessed an unprecedented and, mostly forced, massive migration of Africans out of the continent to various destinations in Asia and the western world—what scholars now recognize as the first phase of the African Diaspora. During this period, it is estimated that five million Africans, mostly from Central and North Africa, were forced to cross the Red Sea and the Indian Ocean for various places in southern and western Asia, including the Middle East. Concurrently, another estimated eleven million Africans, mostly from West Africa, were brought to Europe and the Americas as a result of the transatlantic slave trade (Postma, 2004).

The rate of African emigration slowed during the first half of the twentieth century. Understandably, as the Transatlantic Slave Trade slowly came to an end and the majority of African countries fell under the domination of European colonial regimes, very few Africans were granted permission by the colonial governments to leave home for abroad. The very few who were granted the "privilege" left the continent primarily for further studies and returned to participate in the emerging political process in their various home countries. This trend of slow migration would reverse during the second-half of the twentieth century and initiate what is now known as the second phase of the African Diaspora.

Second Phase of the African Diaspora:

The end of colonial regimes in Africa during the 1950s and 1960s, and the repeal of repressive immigration laws in the United States in 1965 allowed millions of Africans to migrate, mostly voluntarily, to Western Europe, Canada, and the United States. At the time, most Africans saw the West as a place of opportunity, where western education could be obtained to assist in political and economic advancement when they returned to their homelands. However, the sense of optimism that accompanied these new immigrants soon waned as their hope for the eventual voyage home dimmed: deteriorating economic conditions and political instability created by the aftermath of colonization ensured not only that many of these Africans became permanent exiles from their native lands, but also that they were soon followed by millions of others fleeing the same economic hardships, and in many instances, political persecutions as well. Even though exact statistics are scarce, it is estimated that since the 1960s, about five million Africans have left the continent to seek opportunities in Western Europe and North America. This number does not account for Africans living in Asia, South America, Eastern Europe and the Caribbean or the millions of second-generation Africans—children of immigrant parents— who consider themselves African or hyphenated-Africans. Based on the continent's continuous relocation of peoples, the

International Organization for Migration suggests that the African continent currently has the most mobile population of any landmass in the world (2008).

The rate and impact of African immigration remain a topic of debate in academic and political arenas. Academics and policy makers agree that most of the Africans involved in the second phase of the African Diaspora are trained professionals and skilled workers who contribute to the economic development of their adopted countries rather than their countries of birth. This phenomenon, known as a "brain drain," possesses significant problems to the economic and political health of the continent, as it is estimated that "Africa has already lost one-third of its human capital, with approximately 20,000 doctors, academics, engineers, and other professionals leaving the continent annually since 1990" (Shinn, 2002). The United Nations Economic Commission for Africa (ECA) notes, "The emigration of African professionals to the West is one of the greatest obstacles to Africa's development" (2004). The fact remains, however, that while most Africans in exile would love to return home and contribute their knowledge and skills to the development of the continent, political and economic conditions at home have made it almost impossible to return; most professionals who returned to Africa during the 1970s left again due to harsh economic realities and lack of employment and educational opportunities for themselves and their children. Some argue that African exiles send millions of dollars, euros and pounds back to the continent every year, thereby directly and indirectly contributing to the economic development of the continent. However, there is no question that for the foreseeable future, immigration and the loss of human resources to Africa will continue to greatly affect evaluations of economic and political health across the continent.

Effect of Emigration on African Immigrants:

The increasing attention to global immigration leads us to consider another important, but often neglected result: the immigrants themselves. Despite numerous essays and conferences aimed to evaluate the positive and negative effects of immigration on Africa, few have asked the fundamental questions about the quality of life for these African immigrants in their new homes outside the continent. Simply put, how does migration affect the African immigrant? What is life like for these millions of Africans living in exile, voluntary or forced? There is no question that African immigrants face many challenges in their countries of exile: inevitable clashes between cultures that never completely go away, no matter how long a person has lived in a particular place; the constant urge to define and redefine oneself in response to feelings of alienation and not quite being "at home"; and, particularly for new immigrants, the tension of trying to negotiate the old and the new, difference, and loneliness. Coming from countries where black people are often the majority, African immigrants are often for the first time in their lives confronted with "racial categorization and its economic and cultural results in the US [and Western Europe]" (Arthur, 2000). African immigrants are often inexperienced with racial stereotypes about anyone of African descent in these western countries and do not understand that a professional black person may be subjected to the same prejudice as a street vendor (Vesely 2005). Thus, statistics of economic and political impact fail to mark the deep emotional and psychological effect of immigration on the people who have left their family, community, and land of origin. This anthology gives a voice to this silence.

Going Home Again:

While the adage "you can't go home again" is a popular one in western culture, for the people of Africa the understanding is "You must go home again." For many African immigrants, home is only a memory, and they go home as often as they can—on paper and in their thoughts—but not always in reality. The writers in this collection provide visibility and voice to various aspects of these experiences and initiate an already overdue discussion of the topic. Their writings show the effects of Diaspora and illustrate the idea that a cultural scattering brings with it an emotional scattering, a sense that home will never be a place of wholeness anymore. The selections confront the most painful reminders of exile, from not being able to attend the funerals of friends and family members at home to the bitter shock of a newly experienced winter. Many of the writers include images of transportation, echoing the idea that all stability has given way to constant motion. The poems and creative nonfiction in this collection share the common theme of nostalgia, but never in an overly sentimental sense. Some of the pieces are instructive, but never didactic. All of the selections stare into the abyss of exile, searching for scattered pieces of home.

The lyric poem, with its emphasis on emotion, is the chosen outlet for many of the writers, including Padmore Enyonam Agbemabiese, whose work contains deep melancholy mixed with small glimmers of hope. This hope is what pulls the poet into dreams of childhood and the land of his father's birth; these memories provide assurance that he will go home again one day. For Suzannah Mirghani, hope for a new life waits nervously with her before her flight away from home and is later frozen by the cold weather of New York City and London. The weather—gray, damp, and cold—lyrically mimics her lost hope and reminds her even more powerfully of the place she left. Her memories of home taunt her, "Like a jealous lover / Who never treated me properly" ("Home Bound"). No amount of extra clothing can provide the warmth that she left at home. Likewise, the state of Ohio in the United States provides Unoma N. Azuah with no warmth. The starkness of snow reflects the poet's difficulty in adapting to a new set of customs and social boundaries, and she is reminded daily that she is the one who is different. She turns toward the image of a tropical storm—perhaps the opposite of snow—to convey what it feels like to be in exile.

Nicholas Makoha expresses the loss of culture and the absence of a legacy that he fears is inevitable. His work asks the hardest questions, ones that have no answers. Along with his knowledge of the guerrilla forces that ravage his country, he must also face his resentment toward his father. His poetry—a sonnet, a series of couplets and even three-line stanzas, and a narrative poem about his return to Kenya for a funeral—attempts to place order onto the emotional chaos that comes from a diasporic awareness. "A Different World" is the title of one of Rhoda Ndagire Mwanje's poems, but the title could serve all three of her selections equally well. Her poems vividly portray the alienation and loneliness of a person displaced from her home, her culture, and her land. She may have left her country to pursue freedom, but her poems convey emotional imprisonment. In a poem of protest, the directness of Tinashe Mushakavanhu's language contrasts sharply with the lack of direction conveyed in his poetry. Seeing himself as a stray dog, he poignantly shows how his new place of residence has shut him out. His emotional depth transfers well to the personal essay form, in which he tells what it is like to be the only person of color in a racist small town.

Several of the writers in the collection deal with the pain of a loved one's death, and Sheikh Umarr Kamarrah distinguishes between the healing rituals of death within a close community and the complete absence of community when a loved one dies while in exile; without his cultural ceremonies, the poet is left with questions instead of prayers. Everywhere he turns, there is difference. Similarly, Akuba (Grace Quansah) searches for meaning after the death of her cousin, who went to the United States for her education and died, surrounded by strangers. Akuba's lyrical elegy reflects the deepest fear of anyone who sees a relative leave: the promise of a better life becomes instead the end of a life filled with only beauty. Zena Tesfaye-Teferra searches for a recognizable face from home and describes in a narrative poem her experience in a London train station. Every old woman in Ethiopian garments reminds her of her grandmother, and she is the missing child who receives a blessing of spit on the forehead. Her poetry debunks the alluring qualities of constant travel and movement.

Spanning the globe and four centuries, Terhemba Shija weaves magic realism into her poetry to express the diasporic sensibility that the exile will never feel at home and will never find completeness because humankind has destroyed nearly all of creation. Yet she knows she is not truly alone as she pays tribute to the poets who have sought the same ill-fated pursuit. Tolu Ogunlesi's poems attempt to find a point of relation between his home of Nigeria and the busy cities of Europe; however, what he realizes is there are no similarities in the food, in the conversations, or in the pace of life. When he experiences yet another difference, his poetic mindset allows him to imagine home. Language differences can cause an exile to feel even more alone, as Wadzanai Mhute illustrates. In her creative nonfiction, Mhute portrays her interactions with people who cannot pronounce her name and who call her what they want instead of her actual name. She includes a list of instructions that clearly state how not to insult someone with an unfamiliar name, effectively illustrating how closely one's name connects to one's identity.

Also using the expressive form of creative nonfiction, Mansim Okafor relates his personal experiences with racism by way of a social experiment. Upon arriving in the United States, Okafor had heard of the rampant bigotry but did not understand everyone's warnings until he took a job as a janitor. His discoveries provide a lesson not only in race relations but also in class differences. A piece of candy may seem trivial, but as Diarapha Diallo-Gilbert reveals, the widespread usage of a racist name for a confection illustrates the inherent bigotry throughout the culture. Diallo-Gilbert makes it her goal to raise consciousness and to effect change, one piece of candy at a time. Her expository style provides an excellent arena for social activism. The final piece in the collection resonates with the importance of family and cultural traditions. In his creative nonfiction, Vamba Sherif speaks through a first-person narrator in a voice that is quiet and subtle, yet powerful in its storytelling. Sherif concludes with the statement, "Perhaps, I'll return one day."

Perhaps this collection will allow all of us to return home—where we recognize everyone, where we bask in the sunshine, and where we taste, feel, hear, smell, and see everything that we have missed while in exile. Perhaps it will enable us to ask probing questions about our experiences, to share and dialogue about the essence of life in exile. Most importantly, perhaps this collection will help us to not forget who we are and where we come from.

Salome C. Nnoromele
Lisa Day-Lindsey

Poems and Narratives

Padmore Enyonam Agbemabiese

Padmore Enyonam Agbemabiese

Nostalgia

if home

was a bunch of pictures

neatly would I wrap them

beneath my armpit

if the Volta at home

was a drop of liquid

I would bottle enough

for my suitcase

and if the mounts

at home were just grains of sand

I would cup a spoonful

for myself

I would bring them with me

sit them on my lap

to build a treasure in my dreams

to cure nostalgia in my soul

The Smell of Exile

we grew up at home

with a warrior thrust tuning

our souls to sounds of crickets

to rhythms of the soil

to smells of the rivers

knowing large dreams of moonlight joy

we grew up there in an ever rebounding

spirit learning songs of seasons

that dressed our umbilical cords

for the harvest of our dreams—

songs fathers sang in the cycle

many rainless seasons ago

many seasons ago

we walked into the snow sea

waving goodbye to invisible lines

that etched truths of our umbilical cords

into our being into our minds into our hearts

when we heard father died this morning

we were featherless eagles looking

for remnants of our nest among anthills

at a traffic light fragmented by hideous sores

we lost the burial songs golden by a sun

which made the dead sleep like babes

it was here we remembered

the splash of colors, the smell of exile

the poverty of dispossession soaked our souls

they caked memories of green hills

and held us trustees of resentment of things of home

everywhere above our skies locusts burst dams

while the roar of holy water

drowned the glutton voices of our fathers

our blood drank the pus from wounds

buried deep by the locusts beneath the skin

we lost our dreams of a harvest

to the splash of colors

we drowned the songs of our fathers

in the roar of the holy water

there are many seas to cross

with deadly triangular calm

congeal tenacious death breaths

to scream at our tenacious fate

it is only a season ago since we left, yet

we no longer possess the sounds of the crickets

we no longer dance to the rhythms of the soil

what we have is the pus from the wounds

buried deep by the locusts beneath our skin

Prophesy

One day some day
I will claim my wings
I will seize the skies
I will take the land

one day some day
I will return your heart home
I will return your soul to the land
the land of your father's birth

you will return to the land
reading poems of love
from ribbons of human touch
drinking from pools of human laughter

you'll see dreams of amazing grace

one day some day
I will return

return in Waterfalls of Fire

I will return to trembling eyes

step on mounds of burning chaos

pick maggots hanging on mouths

crush the lies in living museums

and the Rainbow won't set

til the poor inherit the kingdom

til the hungry are filled

til they that weep laugh

in the land of their father's birth

Home Again

we venture out of our birthplace,

when we feel we hit the dead end

we wave goodbye to our loved ones

and try to forget some we loved

away from home we celebrate all that's new

but the surprise is the shock and hurt in the new

deep in tears we hear a voice from our past

memories of home come flooding back

soon we tend to forget the new

and wish to go back home again

back at home we realize the past is dead,

we have been away for far too long

One Gentle Night

I saw the moonlight coming out in the dark

and remembered the crickets at home

I cuddled my soul with joy at the moon

but the crickets did not return my song

I raised my head and looked again

it was the floodlights from the street corner

slowly I lowered my head

and thought of my far-away home

The Song

dreams from my childhood

have long passed away

one thing from my childhood I keep

the deep solace of a song

should that ever leave me

let me find death and stay

the songs of my people

are things whose tunes run

in my veins like blood

like the rain on fields of corn

Suzannah Mirghani

Going to America

But what do I know?

I have not yet seen the sun

Beyond rolling West-coast knolls

Apparently, it is much more brilliant

Than any I have ever seen

And will last years longer

Than the dim decades my measly sun could muster

But what do I know?

I have not yet mixed my breath

With the icicle particles

Moving hurriedly on a busy New York street

Apparently, they are more fascinating

Than any other city's winter fantasy

Claiming to be more white in its heart than my city

But what do I know?

I have never been to America

And despite my twenty-eight years

Apparently, I have not yet lived

And my life a meaningless drift

Before this evening and this flight

I board having lost something in the small hours

Suzannah Mirghani

Christmas in London

How I have imagined the winter

How I have tried to feel its cold

Never could I have imagined this

This menace that breaks and enters

And hardens my sick soul

I wrap up in three old odd scarves

I no longer care about the way I look

Or the way they look

Or the way they look at me and laugh

My comforts instincts of survival

About making it to work

And back to my tiny flat

Safely in this chilling dark

Never in my darkest dreams

Have I seen such a starless sky

And never in all my twenty-eight years

Have I been privy to a Christmas night

When the guiding star did not appear

Tonight, the shops can keep their winter line

Keep it tucked away until next winter

I have nothing to give and no one to give it to

I will be fine with my Asda ham and two-pound liquor

I will be fine as long as I can think of her

Home Bound

I know it to be nostalgia

The trick the mind plays

On new geographies

The trick the heart plays

To make me weak

In this new-found-land

Full of possibilities

I know them to be false memories

That keep me thinking of home

And her sun shining brilliantly

I know these to be false memories

If it had always been the case

Why would I otherwise be miles away

In this damp and dingy city?

In the darkness of my sickness

I hear my country call to me

Like a jealous lover

Who never treated me properly

But seeing I had strength to leave

Wanted me back again suddenly

And when I die

I will surface from obscurity

And finally meet the authorities

And be returned to her

In more comfort than I came from her

Either route, I never was free

A bound and docile body on an expensive journey

Nicholas Makoha

In Smoke

I have only had this conversation once.

It was raining, the glass on the window

stained with fingerprints. My back turned

as neighbors played pat-ball in the street.

A purple sky at dusk, clouds dyed grapefruit pink

and you asked, "Aren't you proud to be a Ugandan?"

The silence filled with the laughter from the postman

hiding in the cove of basement flat Talfourd Road

as he smoked imported Dunhill (eight milligram

strength). White plumes crawling up the greystone

finding my nostrils. Every year I have lived here

less of me belongs to my mother's soil. This voice has

lost its song, the tongue, the language. What words

and sounds will I leave for my daughter?

What's on God's Mind?

How many sleepless nights must I tolerate

to avoid dreams being taken away?

In Turi, Africa, I used to

walk across radio waves,

to hear how maize has left the soil

like a battered wife leaves her husband.

My laughter is a swollen lie.

I use the laughter to chase

the memory of my dad from my mind.

It's a dream hidden in the loss of words.

Losing my faith in facts.

Hiding tears in abstracts.

Resenting the days in boarding school

I had to unpack feelings in a stolen jar.

Sitting on school steps

wishing other mothers would steal my heart.

Making jokes to hide the scars.

Humor never erased the pain.

I see my father's streak in my life.

It's why I never look a woman straight in the eye .

Dad lives a flight away

or a phone call my mother will never make.

Their only proof that love exists is me.

The Last Ugandan

It is hard to believe that blood unites a tribe.

My country is landlocked and ruled by guerrilla forces.

Boys are kidnapped to serve as soldiers with guns.

Beneath the mountains of misty Ruwenzori sugar cane

tobacco and cotton grow. Girls are routinely raped and

become sex slaves or "wives" of rebel commanders.

Sometime in the day the light or water will go.

In the paraffin light evenings, curfews begin,

the traditions inherited by past dictators.

My mother bought me a plane ticket to flee Idi Amin.

He was a powerful man loved by many women.

Mum say she sees my father in him.

My Cousin

Kenya was not as green as I remember.

Landing on tarmac that melts to toffee,

my western attire made me a target.

Customs thought me dressed in money

They wanted money and opened my bag;

they wanted money, silence.

I remember my mother screaming on the phone.

I thought she was laughing with her friends.

I grew up with him like a brother, like a son,

lived in his mother's house, did dance routines.

Was there when his father died, became the man.

Two days later we were on a plane.

We'd eat in the room with the gold clock.

At one sitting, eating three meals straight.

Thick Ugali cake and sukamawicke,

that should have lasted a week, we ate it in a day.

Eating loaves of bread just to race,

with Kenyan tea made with milk, not water.

In a stone church with wooden murals,

his body was carried to the side of the altar

as a burden on the shoulders of his cousins.

Friends and acquaintances filled the church,

spilling outside from all doors and exits.

Dignitaries and locals stood side by side.

I went straight to the coffin that lay in the dining room.

I stared at him for ages. Old men held children.

He looked so peaceful; mothers held loved ones

like on school mornings when he couldn't wake.

Everyone carried on like it was just another day.

Lonely tears came later on my return at Heathrow.

Rhoda Ndagire Mwanje

Rhoda Ndagire Mwanje

Kaawa

My woman does not listen to me

She has grown horns like a he-goat

She attended schools of the witty

Many think she is better than me

My Kaawa barks at me, like a dog

I am the intruder, she – the owner

Oftentimes I leap like a frog

In a room that I have long owned

My wife says I am still a child

I must grow and cease to play

We are in a strange land

There is no time to stray

Oh this strange woman

She does not want children

She swallows pills

The way a snake swallows eggs

Why did I never grow up

Why did I never leave my mother's lap

Why did I refuse my father's words

Why am I not a master of letters

My wife says I work like a slave

That I think like a slave

I would love a ready breakfast

She says she works the night shift

Why did I bring her, without a thought

A strange man, in a strange land

My pride, my existence has been put to test

For Kaawa dares to look me in the mouth

Rhoda Ndagire Mwanje

Black Sister

Black sister,

African friend

Why don't you see me?

Why don't you look me in the eye?

And say, Hello

Don't we look alike?

Don't we have the same pain?

Haven't we seen it all?

War

Poverty

Famine

Oppression

Haven't we lived it all?

Escape

Rejection

Humiliation

Powerlessness

Then sister,

Why are we not free?

A Different World

On a morning like this

I would be strolling down a narrow path

On a morning like this

I would be wandering the slopes

Of the Luyima

Skipping pythons, dodging mambas

To collect firewood

And sit by the fireside with somebody

To cook matooke with ntula and dodo.

But I'm here today

Locked between now and then

Watching as the winter darkness

Entices the trembling light of the day

Watching through my glass window

Busy automobiles rush to nowhere

Yet a terrible loneliness numbs my limbs

And today

I know the difference

Tinashe Mushakavanhu

Tinashe Mushakavanhu

Stray Dog

i am an exile in wales, the black apparition

darting along the one-way king street in carmarthen

my past lies far   far behind me

it is this diaspora route i have taken, but no

it has bilingual signposts that do not speak my language

nothing points back

        where i came from

life is not a straightforward highway with signposts giving
directions

        warning: it has NO EXIT

life is a black stray dog searching for shelter in this rain

        it is me

Inside Outside:
The Politics of Exile

Every day I ask myself, what am I—an African of many generations, a Zimbabwean child—doing here in Wales, when I am reminded daily that I don't belong? What am I doing here, away from the sun-drenched plains of Africa in this dank and cold climate? What am I doing among the sometimes indifferent Welsh people who understand nothing whatever of *ubuntu*? Every day, I feel the pain of separation from my true home and from family and friends left behind in poor, blighted Zimbabwe, a beautiful land vice-gripped by an utterly selfish and totally corrupt dictator who is as much a curse to his country as Idi Amin, Augusto Pinochet or Slobodan Milosevic were ever to theirs.

I hate it but we have been fleeing our country to live in other places, among people who do not have full sympathy with us; people who accuse us of crimes we should have committed and crimes we have no intention to commit. I thought Wales had all the answers to rest my heart upon. But who you are is always determined by where you are. The bigotries of Wales weigh on me sometimes. I have met condescension in the eyes of bank clerks and shop attendants and malign intent in store detectives watching me along the aisles picking my groceries. No. Fact. If anybody should be scared around here, it's me. I am often the only black person surrounded by a sea of over-caffeinated people; flabby, pale, ill-proportioned figures so common here. I hate it when I have to negotiate my place all the time because of who I am. Yes, I may not be facing the tyranny of poverty and politics back in Zimbabwe, but I have to constantly look out for myself to survive in this new place. Perhaps it's just me with a jaundiced perception of this world.

One in every three black girls on the street is a nurse. Yes, one of those in starched white uniform. Or is it blue? It seems to me all our black sisters ever seem to do here is to become nurses or care workers. I thought this place was supposed to be full of endless opportunities but they always seem to narrow down to petty, greasy kitchen jobs, till operators, janitors, and waiters.

Here in Carmarthen, a small market town, south-west of Wales, the only black face I am used to seeing every day when I wake up is mine. I am getting used to the curious stares. I am the odd one out everywhere I go. I am different. There is always baggage that comes with that, this feeling that you're constantly on display, being judged and stereotyped and never knowing quite how people feel about you.

It becomes terribly lonely when every day the newspapers carry the most hysterical nonsense about black Africa. I had never really come to terms, I suppose, with my blackness—I had never particularly noticed that I was black—and it was something of a shock suddenly to realize that my skin for the Welsh was a natural label that reads Asylum Seeker, Refugee, Mugabe, Inferior. The black not only fights racism but actually digs out from himself that necessary foxhole of self-respect which everyone needs on this battleground of a supposedly multiracial Wales. I find it very much a place where the colour and shade of your skin and the texture of your accent matters.

The loneliness of exile, far from home and in a hostile surrounding, brings those who live far from their homes closer together. A "black laager" mentality develops which is cultivated and flourished in places like the Africa Centre in Swansea. There we are always, people drawn together by the likeness of our skin and no more. As we sit there in the safety of numbers and in the anonymity of educated talk which the beer readily stimulates, I can see how wretched our position is, always having to form a laager against the hordes of white locals. It is not enough for us to heed Aimé Césaire and Leopold Sedar Senghor's call to be black and proud and beautiful; little teeth of uneasiness always gnaw at our self assurance for there is no answer to a white man's sneer.

Exile is so demoralizing. We are all changed. We all don't come on like we used to do back home. I mean everyone looks phony and suspicious and cynical and there's no black feeling among us anymore. We're all scraggy at the seams. And everyone seems to individualize themselves so much that even the sour comradeship that's still there really leaves a reek of sewage disposal systems. What's happened to us? What happens to us black Africans in exile? We stand each to each like cities beyond repair. Shelley's "Ozymandias" has really come among us. When black people meet there's always an element of sizing each other up. We speak with our eyes. Where do you come from? What brought you here? Questions we never answer. We are all colored with prejudices. Nigerians are conmen. Zimbabweans are hungry and desperate cowards. Somalis and Ethiopians and Sudanese are refugees.

There are times I have been made to realize I am in the backyard of white men and their kind of law. On a balmy Sunday afternoon while I was taking a lazy walk down-town, a police patrol car suddenly reduced speed to move in tow with me, the eyes of its occupants scanning my dark presence, accusing me of a crime I was not planning to commit. It suddenly struck me that everybody I knew was white: my work colleagues, my classmates, right down to the nurses at the hospital. It paralyzed a part of me, realizing that I was on an island that contained millions of whites who whenever they chose were all suddenly against me. It was so unreal it had to be real. I could have stood up in attention at that moment shouting Guilty! Guilty! Guilty! But all I did was pretend they were not there. Maybe I was just a shadow lurking among their fears.

I just started laughing long and loud. (My degree of madness becomes more apparent at such moments). There is often no mirth in the sounds. I just laugh. People hurry past me afraid to meet my eyes for fear I am a reckless black drunkard who is mad/paranoid/delusional. At least I know, I only have one thing they will never have. My mother's tongue. I have a language they don't have. I can speak and write and dream and defecate in their language, but here Shona is my language, mine and mine alone. Sometimes, I want to call out and say to them, *Murikunditarisirei? Munondiziva here? Mutupo wangu munouziva here? Ndati murikunditarisireiko? Siyanai neni mhani?*

And for all the years I have lived in Wales, I have learnt, almost on each occasion I speak to a white person, that my accent is no good. That I do not pronounce the vowels in the English English way. I am always humiliated each time I am asked what I am saying, or if I could speak in English, please, even though I would be speaking in English. Sometimes I resort to spelling the word I was trying to say, only for the other person to show some excitement, when they think they now understand what I am saying, and go like, "Oh, you meant 'LIBRARY'? Sorry I didn't catch that…", or sometimes a by-stander would come to my rescue and explain to the other what he or she thinks I am saying, "I think he means that…." These are always embarrassing times for me, [yes] a first class English graduate who suddenly realized that I did not speak English very well, even though I was born with the incestuous language that was always competing with my mother's tongue – Shona.

I once made a mistake of going out with a white girl[friend] into a pub. It's never safe to presume that the Welsh are not racist. I remember a haunted hush greeted us and male eyes pierced through my soul with a kind of reproach that violently said motherfucker you are now growing too big for your pants. White guys don't like it when you get along with one of their girls, the same guys who have been able to do what they wish with black women for so long. There's something very odd about it, even suicidal; if you go around telling your women to stay away from me because I am sexually potent, and you in the mean time are on the other side of town with all the black girls you can find. It is very strange, that we black men represent a personal, sexual, psychological threat for white men. Of course we stayed, had one drink each and walked out. I expected a group of them to follow us and beat the blackness out of my skin. They didn't bother. No bleach can do that. Michael Jackson failed the test.

What is baffling is their general ignorance. There is no Africa in their curriculum. There is no Africa in their imagination. Africa is one big village. There is no difference between Zimbabweans and Nigerians and Kenyans. We are just the same. I was approached in a coffee shop by an elderly [gentle]man who wanted to know if I knew a friend of his Abduwari Azziz from Morocco. I said I didn't know. I come from Zimbabwe and I have never been to North Africa. Oh, Rhodesia, you mean. Zimbabwe-e, damn it, I wanted to shout back as the old [gentle]man said it as a matter of fact. Yes, that's right. There are some people who still live in the past, those whose minds are still tuned backwards, those who refuse to accept the present in its present context.

I don't wish to stay in exile forever and at the same time I don't want to return to the poverty and tyranny back home. It is hard to live in that repressive state. I left because I wanted to see more of life, but my stay is not indefinite. It is temporal. My visa to stay expires. Thinking of going back home terrifies me and yet I can't stop thinking about it. In this day and age, home is often not far from where you are – it reaches out to you via email, text messages and Facebook. The problems and images are so real and immediate. The deterioration obvious. My peers can't wait their turn to leave. Everyone is leaving.

This continuous bleeding that every month takes away the youngest, the boldest and, why not say it, the most talented, is proof that the well being of the people is not the center of attention of the Zimbabwean government. Political elements, ideology, and past evidence of loyalty are prioritized above the "here" and "now" of people's needs. As long as "up there" they don't recognize that they haven't been able to build a country where people want to stay and use their energies, the problem of emigration will not be solved.

How many will have to leave so that we can hear the phrase, "We failed, we haven't been able to give a future to Zimbabweans." I suspect, because I know the hard-headedness that comes with too many years in power, that not even this desolated postage stamp of a landlocked country full of tired and aged people, with their children living in other latitudes, will make the Zimbabwean government come to reason. I imagine the accusations of "sold to imperialism" and "traitor" that will be heard these days in the Institute of Radio and Television.

I keep wondering how things are going to turn out. Nothing promises to be better. I can see it is going to be a long time before any good news comes from home. Memories of home do not fade, no matter where we go. What we think is what we are and what we are is what we think. Perhaps…

memories are stubborn stains

etched on my face

memories are scars

that run deep my bosom

memories are stitches

that keep me together

whole

Sheikh Umarr Kamarah

Sheikh Umarr Kamarah

Death in Exile

Death:

A call we are bound to heed

An incident that must happen to us

A state inevitable

That all must experience

That is what it seems to me now

As a child

Death was the rare vocabulary

That made my parents sad and subdued

Tears oozing freely

From their old eyes

Down their tired cheeks

I did not understand it then

But now…

Death:

An every minute reality

56

Is a community affair

Family and friends gather

The dead is never alone

Ceremonies are performed

Prayers said in the community's way

The ancestors fully notified about

The coming of their own

Earth will prepare her bed

To receive her own

In the soil of his or her land

The dead is laid to rest

But…Death in Exile:

The body of my childhood friend expired

In America

A soul in exile

Away from home

Across the turbulent Atlantic

My friend's corpse is trapped

Death in exile

Emptiness, loss, loneliness

No family

No ceremonies

The soil is foreign

The casket is Alien

The prayers are different

Will the Ancestors cross the Atlantic?

Will they receive my friend?

Yesterday, Death arrested my parents

No visitation allowed

Away from "home"

I wept in exile

Could not wail like I would

In Africa

My next door neighbor cannot be disturbed

With a pillow on my "refugee" mouth

I contained the "noise," or

911 will wipe my tears with handcuffs

When the ceremonies are over

Everyone asks for

The child in exile

The child who cannot witness The Burial of his parents

A Lost Generation

Here I am

Lost in thought…ruminating?

My country lingers…a forceful feeling

A feeling of nostalgia

Imprisoned in a deep sea of thoughts

A feeling of impotence invades my whole self:

Here I am

Once a native

A native of my birthplace…now

An alien in the U.S.

A documented alien—sounds respectable?

"Do you like it here?"

"No," I replied.

"Well, why are you here?"

"My country can't take me; well…

No, no, ah, ah, I can't take my country."

"Which is which?"

"I am confused."

Singing in Exile

A wide sheet of water

I on one side

They on the other

Like a plastic wrapper

On the sole of a walk-about

I am to my memories…

Fresh water

calm waves kissing the banks

quenching my thirsty feet

buried in mountains of tropical sand

evening sea breeze

squeezes through thick strands

in the forest of my head

chasing away innocent grains of sand

picking bubbles of sweat

off the tree of my body

feeling at one with a calm ocean

On their way home

birds sing of their day's exploits

bats perform a ritual of circles

announcing a new-found pasture

a happy army of pigeons

to the East swing

singing of fresh corn

Another wave falls on my sandy feet

the water returns to the ocean

my feet hug a new layer of wet sand

my hand skates over

the golden grains

from toe to heel

my eyes on the hill

enveloped in a green hue

overlooking the sandy beach

where children play

uninhibited naked free safe

clean grains on their heads

cling to parts of the body

gently falling off

as they run back and forth

chasing a wild ball

parents watch and smile

adults swim

talk laugh eat play

husbands stealing a glance

at a well-endowed passing lady

wives ignoring male temptations

packed in tight briefs

surrounded by muscles

singing of power

Another wave falls on my feet

wakes me up

It is CNN world report:

Sierra Leone...

rebel war

death poverty disease hunger

flourishing on diamonds.

Today's mail:

Visa, American Express, Sears, Master Card

a wealth of credit cards

a letter from Home amidst junk mail.

CNN world report has just ended

a child amputee on the screen

News of my country!

Refrains of old

slowly creep into

my crammed memory

mixed, one with another

all striving for ascendancy:

"My lovely Elizabeth"

"Memuna"

"'I can see clearly now the rain is gone"

"Oh, how good it used to be,"

Songs of yesterday…

Other lines lost

A World Lost.

Zena Tesfaye-Teferra

Westward

I had seen her on the pavement…

Her head bobbing in a halo of white.

The crowded street pushed all the heads together,

welding the pedestrian sea into a multi-headed dragon.

It implements its will disguised as signs and directions:

Stop! Go! Lights blink and chime,

adding sonar violence to polluted stale-smoky air.

The dragon inched east on a busy London thoroughfare

An anomaly, an alien,

she stood still facing a shop window, her back to the
        dragon's tail.

I too was stationary on an escalator folding into land.

The others ran. Even to steady descent, they rushed.

They pushed. They shoved.

A head knocked my suitcase,

spilling the contents: Empty

A few changes of clothes, books, and cassette tapes…

strewn soundlessly, heralded my arrival.

The head ran on, presently chained to the mass dragon,

incognizant it had unpacked me.

Crouched to gather the issue of my case,

I caught the reflection of her ghostly white dress.

My suitcase full again I ran toward her

She was an elderly Ethiopian, a sage at hand,

pointing back at a haughty mannequin as though contesting.

Her long white dress colorfully embroidered at the hem,

back straight, she defied direction. Defied definition.

I caught up with her "Emma, Emmama!" lifting my voice

"Maereye!" my sweet! she cries as though she knew me!

Tenderness

we embrace then kiss. Cheek to cheek to cheek.

She smiles cracking her moon face ablaze,

nine plaits follow the length of her cranium;

to gush at her nape completing the halo.

Her tattooed neck meets her ear lobes,

where golden globes rest balancing her eyes.

A white shawl covers her head rendering her otherworldly

She could have been from recently demoted Pluto.

Or an Arab. A Hindu. A Fulani. Demotions apply equally.

"You look like my grandmother," I sob, at once song and dirge.

As I kneel, the mannequin's pointing finger lowers in shame.

The heads are mostly deaf to us. But not blind.

My suitcase cowers as heads keep bumping it, but does not
   spill.

It has no issues

…"May God bless you, lead you to greener pastures,"

she rains gentle spit on my forehead – sealing her utterance.

My tears are violent edging south to her feet.

Clip, clop…I imagine the policeman on his horse, passing.

"Ma'am, the Thames does not accept salty African rivulets."

I am afraid, certain we are breaking with British norms.

The northern bound train screeches… It's waiting for me.

London shrugs, slighted by my final departure.

Washington is waiting up in arms. A welcome wave?

Transient sounds sexy but even a city resents the bestowal
   of its honor.

I am leaving the U.K. for the U.S. Exchanging one consonant
for another.

I read the law for three years in Wiltshire.

Ten years later, I am still illegal in Virginia.

Swarthy does not illuminate Lady Liberty's torch

Now I spill my tears in the Potomac, but it grew wide on
African tears.

Though blessed by a sage, the green dollar does not a
green card make.

I am only free to labor, depositing my youth in illegal
installments.

I offer my sweet sage-scented sweat, shooting pain from
my knees.

Unlawful exchanges between hand and mouth. One. Two.

Three grandparents, I left behind. I pack again.

If I start now, I will make it to this last one's funeral

Wadzanai Mhute

What's in a Name?

I am Zimbabwean and live in the United States, which prompts me to ask this question: What's in a name? Shakespeare said, "A rose by any other name would smell as sweet." This is what I consider when I tell my mom that I want to change my name. WADZANAI is my name and I bet you cannot pronounce it. It sounds the way it looks; just sound it out and there you have it. WAH-DZUH-NUHYEE. Yet I have heard all sorts of interpretations, this after I have breathed in slowly and said it out loud.

"Huh?" is usually the first response.

Then: "Wuh who?"

"Whatsa what?"

My favorite: "No, what's your name?" (Slowly as if I am mentally challenged).

I usually respond, "My *name* is Wu-dzuh-nuhyee."

"Oh! I thought..."

Yeah, you thought wrong.

Watzanaaai? Wadzeenuyi? What's a night? Wednesday night?

No, it's...

"Well, I'll just say Whatsanight to help me remember."

"Don't you have a shorter/another name?"

No, if I did, would I put myself through this torture?

Then I thought that I would shorten it at work. People look at my "Wadza" name badge and say "Wa-who? Can I just call you Wanda?"

No, you may not!

I see it coming. They begin by saying, "My name is...," and they look at me expectantly, hand extended. You can imagine how I tense up and dread the inevitable (after an awkward pause): "What's your name?"

I breathe in slowly, then say it. Ready for a witty response. Ready to be a good sport even though I have had five years of this and cannot tolerate it much more. I once attended a Zimbabwean fundraising event in Atlanta. At the registration desk the Zimbabwean girl asked for my name, I automatically began to spell it, and she stopped me in mid-sentence. "Just tell me what it is. I can spell it, you know."

"Oh sorry, it's just that..." I began to explain.

She cut me off. "Your name?"

"Wadzanai."

"So what's so hard about that?"

I tried to explain again.

"Surname?"

"Mhute."

She spells M-U-T-E.

Lord have mercy.

"It has an H. That's why I spell it because most people get it wrong."

"Well, you said it like you were American. It's MOOTE! I know how to spell that."

She waves me aside and asks my friend her name.

"Tambu Moyo."

"See," she says to me. "She says her name properly."

I think about this for a minute; maybe it's the way I have been pronouncing it. Maybe I should pronounce it so the meaning is evident in Shona. Though who pronounces their name that way? Besides when I have done so, it's simply interpreted as my accent mispronouncing words so the name is remixed.

"Wuhdzuneyi?"

My sister always gets that; her name is Tendai—TEN-DUH-YEE. Nine out of ten people say it back to her. "TEN-DEY."

So no, it wouldn't make a difference. Besides even after that, the closest anyone has come is "Wah? Tzanayi?" as if my name is a question.

Then there was this guy I liked. When my friend introduced us, he asked for me to spell my name (not many ask me that, by the way; I highly recommend it).

He said it several times and asked if he was saying it correctly. Wow, I could have married him; actually anyone who makes the effort instantly becomes my life long friend. He gave me an idea: if I want to measure a guy's interest, he has to respond in a similar way. While I love and even want to hug anyone who hears my name and nods without comment even though they do not know what I just said and cannot be bothered, guys I like who do that? Forget it. "Not interested" is what they unwittingly say and I get the message. What a foolproof system! (Unless, of course, they do not wish to offend me or are afraid they did not hear me properly and do not want to admit it, you are forgiven!)

My name means "Unite, get together." I wish it was "Leave me alone, get away, far, far away." My last name MHUTE, even Zimbabweans either spell it or pronounce it wrong. They usually mistake it for the common MUTI which means tree. My last name means "Mist or fog," one I would love to disappear in when someone asks for my name.

Advice when you meet someone with a name you cannot pronounce.

1) **Do** ask for a spelling.
2) **Do** ask them to repeat it s-l-o-w-l-y.
3) **Do** show interest, ask what it means.
4) **Don't** ask for a shorter version.
5) **Don't** ask for another name or an "easier" name or a "Christian" name—in short, **DON'T**; it's offensive.

"That's pretty" is a common response, which I interpret as "That's unusual," because it's usually preceded by confusion in the face, a nervous smile, then....yeah, right!

With all this drama you can imagine my great willingness to change it. As my luck would have it, I do not have a second name. My older brother has three, my sister and younger brother have two but me? One was enough. So when people ask for my other name, the answer is "I don't have one!"

I love the name Anesu, meaning "God is with us." It also sounds simple enough to pronounce. I tried it at work.

"A-who? Thought your name was whatsanight?"

"Ans-what?"

Sigh. Forget it!

"Yeah, it's whatsanight!"

Mansim Okafor

This Air Is Damp with Bigotry

I have always prayed to be in this country, the USA. The reasons for this desire will make a whole book. Suffice it to say that it started with a Dumez bulldozer uprooting a giant tree and surrounding it was a bunch of adults singing that people should come and see an American wonder. Did they know that Dumez was a French company? With hindsight, I now know two other things: the "caterpillar" driver was definitely French, and none of the "praise singers" had a clue which country made the bulldozer. To them, anything strong (the bulldozer and the driver) and beautiful (Elizabeth Taylor et. al.) must come from that great country. That day, I got inoculated.

So, as I sat, waiting to be interviewed for a student visa at the U.S. embassy along Abayomi Street, Lagos, I felt like someone in a trance. The possibility that an unknown entity like me should get this far to my dream country was beyond comprehension. How I received admission into graduate school with a scholarship to boot will be a story for an entirely different day. I was so consumed in thought to notice a middle-aged man who waited by my side. I jumped as I noticed him, and we exchanged pleasantries. He soon learned I was going to the United States for the first time.

"Young man, pay attention to what I'm gonna tell you and you gonna do well in the States," he addressed me like a drill sergeant to a platoon of recruits. "They'll be looking for an opportunity to nail you," he insisted without bothering to explain who the "they" were. "Always remember that the white man does not like you. And, they will show it whenever they have the opportunity. Therefore, do not give them that opportunity. The very first day you enter any place, anyone who wanted to steal from there will do so because they know you will be the first and the only suspect. So, for the very first weeks, try not to go into the lab or office with a bag. Make sure you are not the first inside a building, lab, office, or classroom. Make sure you are not the last to leave. If you come before every other person, stay in the lobby or corridor until others arrive. Always keep your hands in your pockets when you enter any office or lab. Keep away from the girls, from parties, from the police, and from the courts. Use the main highways—avoid side streets. I believe you will make it if you take my advice," he added just before he responded to a call for the holder of the number fourteen ticket.

Whoa! Was I going to "the promised land," or was I headed to war in a desert of scorpions? But how could the latter possibly be? For heaven's sake, I was headed to "God's own country" and not to a concentration camp. He must have had a traumatic experience that generated this mindset of siege. What exactly happened? I could not ask him since he was long gone and could be seen arguing furiously with the counselor in Booth #13. I did not know anyone could argue with a counselor and still live. But not only was my embassy friend doing serious battle with that lady behind the cage, he appeared to be holding his own. Soon word began making the rounds that Counselor Number 13 was the embassy's paid executioner. Yet, my embassy friend did not only survive that encounter, he flashed his approved document as he passed me while still cursing, "The frustrated witch derives satisfaction from torturing poor Nigerians who do not know their full rights." Something told me that this type of man was a born troublemaker. From what I saw of him, I began to suspect that most of his advice was derived from a mind meticulously groomed for mischief.

I looked up after he left and saw Counselor Number 13

staring at me. How could I tell her I did not know the "idiot"? In my culture, it was irrelevant whether I did or not; giving audience to an opponent attracted serious censure. I felt my end had come when my number came up and I was to report at Booth #13.

She smiled as I came up, and my heart stopped. She kept smiling as she flipped through a couple of my papers, asked a couple of questions, and got my answers from a trembling pair of lips, all punctuated with "madam." She smiled broadly at the end, and wished me a lucky stay in her country. It looked like a miracle. What? So, she did not hold it against me that I spoke with her "enemy"? Hmmm! This was more like the "America of Roy Rogers," a country where good people are spared the trauma of unfair punishment. After all, a country that made the "caterpillar" of my childhood could not be inhabited by minds that hold grudges. Whatever was the case, my experience at the embassy told me that the "they" apparently did not include all white women. I wished I could run into my "embassy friend" and tell him things might not be as bad as he tried to make it. But as I left the embassy, visa in hand and the dream of America now more real than my beating heart, the only thing in my mind was to get back to the Ofili-Okonkwos, my sister-in-law and her husband. They needed to know that the gamble they started had struck a jackpot. And I needed to call my wife, and my mother, and my friends, and…my third cousins.

For inexplicable reasons, the advice of my embassy friend managed to bubble to the top immediately I came face to face with my first "mortal enemy" on American soil, the immigration officers at JFK International Airport in New York. All the goodwill of the counselor at Booth #13 was faded memory so dim it seemed like a dream in last year's sleep. I swallowed hard. A black man of immense size, he took my papers and looked at my face. He nodded.

"You, a professor?" he asked in obvious admiration.

"Yes, sir," I answered, having been told by a friend that university lecturers were called professors in America.

"What do you teach?"

"Physiology, sir."

"Man, those equations are too much for my head," he confessed, sheer admiration written all over his face.

"You remember some, you struggle with others," I informed him, having concluded it was useless telling him that physiology was light years away from physics.

"Welcome to our country," he finally said. "Hope you enjoy your stay."

I thanked him and was soon on my way. Along the way, I struck off all black male Americans from the "they" my embassy friend spoke about. Not knowing my left from my right, I found a convenient chair, sat down, and tried to absorb the grandeur of the place. Soon, a restaurant opposite beckoned, and I obliged. The menu obviously was foreign. Trying to avoid eating things I do not know, I opted for a couple of "apples" I saw on the shelf.

"You want those?" the young man there asked.

"Yes, sir."

"They are not apples, they are peaches," he informed me.

"Are you just coming from the fatherland?"

"Yes."

"Boy, I've been dreaming to get there some day," he confessed.

"Great place," I managed to say.

"I want to breathe fresh air, and watch those elephants and lions and tigers playing around," he sang on with euphoria.

"Yes, it's usually a beautiful sight," I added, not knowing how to tell an adult that wildlife does not really roam that freely in Africa. "And, how much is the 'apple'?"

"No, brother, that is my gift for a fellow brother from the home country."

A fellow brother from the home country? A gift from a perfect stranger on my very first day in America? This was more like the America of my childhood, where Roy Rogers hunted down bad men and saved young women. I was now convinced that the "they" excluded all black American males. I wish I could run into my embassy friend and advise him to go drink the river.

My good fortune continued at my final destination, Wayne State University, an oasis of serenity within the wilderness of blight. For the first two days, I walked about Scott's Hall, the School of Medicine complex, with my hands neatly buried in my pants pockets. That soon proved unnecessary because the faculty and staff, mostly white, were unbelievable. Probably aware of the peculiar problems with foreign students, they had the goodwill to make allowances for inherent deficiencies that trailed people like me from home. Of course, I spoke funny. Besides, as my friends and family had always complained, I "swallowed" some of my vowels and, sometimes, whole words. The community was very accommodating. Dr. Yingst, my supervisor, and Ms. Ginny Barrett, the lab technician, were always apologizing whenever they wanted me to repeat something I said. When it became obvious that I could not use the computer or type, Dr. Ram, the professor in charge of my first major lab, made a clear distinction between the academic merit of a submission and the packaging. Though he would have preferred it typed, he allowed me to submit my labs in long hand until I could master word processing. My experience at Wayne State University was so pleasant that I had to exclude all white males from the "they" list.

After graduate school, I got a Postdoctoral Research

Fellowship at the Lions Eye Research Institute of the University of Louisville. Though a wonderful place, research soon became so monotonous I could feel myself slowly drifting into depression. I threw everything at my morbid foe to no avail. One day, I was busy pouring my mind out to a friend and colleague, Dr. Sherry Ball , when it dawned on me that I had once been an author. Yes, I had a scrappy book, *Chinelo*, credited to my name and, I guess, that makes me an author! I started writing later that night. Three-hundred pages into a new book, *Rainbows on Angel Wings*, I became aware of a serious deficiency in one of the scenes. A section dealing with ethnic discrimination appeared to lack enough emotional essence necessary to make it believable. I sought help from a friend who, in my opinion, was a guru on such issues. Based on his stories, every act of injustice ever known to man has been done to Mike! It is either that Mike never forgets any injustice, or his entire being attracts racially-based unkindness like a huge magnet. It is possible that he made up some of those stories; hence, my scientific mind always left a couple of question marks on each story and double asterisks at the end.

"You are a lucky man," Mike insisted after I told him I have never experienced racial discrimination here in America. "Not even in Detroit?"

"No."

"Not here in Louisville?"

"No."

"Well, your college degree insulates you from some of the shit that we go through in this society." Mike was emphatic in his animated way. "If you were a janitor, a black janitor, you would see the true color of this country."

"I don't know whether I want to see anything," I insisted. "Just tell me how it feels and that will be sufficient for what I am doing."

"My brother, it defies description—it just kills you as a person," he deadpanned, drawing leisurely from his Camel cigarette. "I just can't explain it. You have to experience it in order to feel it."

On a dare, the type that nearly exterminated my ancestors, I went looking for employment at a cleaning company. MasterClean, a modest outfit at the Bluegrass Industrial Parkway, was my first port of call. A middle-aged man, whom I later learned was the top manager, welcomed me politely into his office. Apparently reading my life history from the battered front of my 1985 Toyota Cressida, he felt I was an out-of-luck man in search of a temporary job to tide me over difficult times. He, a white man, was sympathetic or, at least, projected that image. He gave me a generous rate and good hours. He said I should not hesitate to come to him if I needed help. He even promised to find me a management position if one opened up soon. I was impressed. He soon handed me over to my group manager, a peppy, pretty lady who needed to keep an eye on her diet. She was strictly business-like. That was okay with me until she announced a pay rate one dollar lower than what the top manager had given me. Of course, I protested.

"We cannot pay you different from the others," the black lady insisted, "and if that is not okay with you, you are free to go."

Of course, I did not leave. Didn't I come to witness discrimination? So, what was my problem? Why leave this early when my experiment with the mop was yet to begin? In fact, I should be enjoying my preliminary data. But, was this actually discriminatory or was she just an efficient subordinate trying to save her company some money? I then remembered a sad experience I had with another black lady back in Detroit. Could it be that my embassy friend meant the black lady? How could that possibly be?

She immediately assigned me to my site supervisor, Kevin. Something told me that she had talked to Kevin concerning my hours because that was the first thing Kevin addressed when I arrived.

"Nobody gets paid for four hours here," Kevin informed me flatly. "You may want to look for another job if that is not okay with you."

"But…"

"You can go now," he promptly dismissed me.

No, I did not go. Instead, inwardly fulfilled, I insisted that I really needed to keep the job. Apparently satisfied, Kevin took me to one cavernous wing of Chi Chi's corporate headquarters, handed me a bunch of keys that opened only that wing, and told me what to do. I immediately went to work and when I was done, promptly locked up and left. Back in my car, I entered all my experience into a logbook, smiled, and drove home.

The next day, Kevin was livid with anger. He wanted to know why I left without finishing my work. I insisted that I did finish my work. He then took me to another wing of the office complex and said I did not clean that wing the previous day. Suspecting foul play, I immediately brought out my bunch of keys and proved to him that none of the keys could open the new wing. Oh, it was his error—he had meant to assign both wings to me but forgot! That was how my cleaning duty got doubled, and within the following five weeks, the lobby and the CEO's office were added to it without a commensurate increase in hours and hourly rates. By this time, I was beginning to feel exploited. What type of person treats a fellow man like an animal, and not any other animal but a beast of burden? Had Kevin been white, I would have attributed his obvious exploitive predisposition to some form of racial bias. But he was not, thus limiting my choices to inelegant interpretations that gave me little satisfaction.

Incidentally, I had no way of knowing whether a white supervisor would have treated me better. Since I clean the corporate headquarters of an international organization, I wondered whether the staff of the company, an apparently more sophisticated group, would be more sensitive to the emotions of the "lowly ones" in their midst, such as the poor janitor. This question was answered on my fifth week on the job when, for the very first time, I met light pouring through an open door. I suspected someone was working late. On my previous visits to that room, I had seen a framed picture of a middle-aged white lady. She must be a single mother since I had not seen the picture of a man there even though a picture of a teenage girl hugged hers at an intimate and enviable angle.

I approached the room with caution, making as much noise as possible so as to alert the room's occupant of my approach. She appeared to have acknowledged my presence because she started talking to me even before I got there. But there was a problem—she addressed me as Nancy, probably the name of the previous janitor. She bolted upright when my frame appeared by the door. Ignoring my greeting, she showed on her face that she resented my presence there.

"Don't go there," she stooped me as I made for her trash can.

"But I need…"

"Just stay out and I'll bring it over," she said slowly with an exaggerated sense of politeness as she quickly moved over to the trash can, handed it over to me, and shut the door behind her. "Leave the can by the door," she instructed, this time faster.

I leaned by the door feeling like dirt. My first reaction was to leave the overfilled trash can by the door where I stood. But on second thought, I remembered I was on a study. In the study, this sort of experience should not only be tolerated with all humility, it should be welcomed. I nodded and moved on. This time, I remembered the advice of my embassy friend. Maybe, I reasoned, I might have been too quick in removing white women from the "they" list. That night, I officially reinstated them in my diary. For the next four days, she dropped her trash can by the door; I emptied it and left the clean can by the door. That experience did not kill me as Mike had suggested, but it did something to my soul that made that wing of the building look different. The air also smelled evil.

Two days after this experience, I was just entering the kitchen area, glass cleaner and paper towel in hand, when a young man entered. I greeted him and he nodded without a word. He poured himself some coffee and turned to go while I busied myself cleaning the sink and the faucet.

"What are you doing here?" a voice echoed behind me.

"Cleaning."

"You are not supposed to come in here," he informed me, his face serious, eyes ablaze and threatening violence.

My spirit simply died! Did he mean what I thought he meant? I had just told him I was the janitor, so what was so difficult to understand in that? Then, I remembered — I had an accent buried in a deep, croaky voice. And I have been accused of "swallowing" some of my words. Maybe he did not fully understand me.

"I... am...the...ja-ni-tor," I enunciated as slowly and as clearly as my bubbling temper could allow, half a dozen puffs of steam escaping my nose as I spoke, as I watched him zoom off like an addled deer.

Just then, I remembered Mike. How could anybody possibly describe the feeling of rape, meshed in rage, mixed with shock, and buried in hopelessness? One could kill for that, or one could go the opposite direction and wallow in perpetual depression. The whole atmosphere immediately smelled of sulfur. I also remembered my embassy friend.

Maybe the white man ought to come back to the "they" list.

I went over to the janitorial room and rummaged for a cigarette even though I did not smoke. I would have smoked dope if I had laid hands on some, any type. I went outside to clear my head. What did he mean by saying I was not supposed to be there? Janitors cleaned the place, so it couldn't have meant that janitors were not supposed to be there. Maybe he had mistaken me for a black man who worked for the company and who was not supposed to be in that wing of the office complex. Even at that, his face and eyes betrayed a streak that was not required for that singular purpose. Besides, he saw me with cleaning materials and I told him I was cleaning. What was difficult to understand in that? It felt more like he was insinuating that only some types of janitors were allowed in that section; it felt more like racial discrimination. Whoa! I have just been discriminated against; I felt like dancing, but it was just too painful. I had to remind myself that I was in an experiment that appeared to have worked. Mike was sort of right: some people will treat you like trash if you lived by taking out trash. At this point, I felt I had had enough. I was confident I could write the problematic scene in my book better and with ease. My mission accomplished, I was ready to give notice of quitting the job when providence gave me a bonus.

As a compliment to the main manager who offered me the job, the white man that was nice to me, I gave two weeks' notice instead of just dropping out of sight as is common with this type of job. A week into the notice, the new management of the building complex called a meeting of all the cleaners. They were not happy with the job we were doing. All tiers of MasterClean management were there. Afraid they were about to lose their franchise, we were warned not to say a word to the building management, no matter what they said. The area manager was to handle all the questions and issue instructions to us. Everything went well until the manager of the building complex solicited questions from us, the lowly cleaners.

My hand went up, and I could see all my managers clutch their hearts.

"Sir," I started politely. "I work in some other place. Whenever my supervisor has a problem with something in that place, he would invite the person involved and address the issues directly with him. I clean the CEO's office, the lobby, and wings D and E. Do you have problems with any one of these areas?"

"To be sincere with you, no."

"Thank you," I said with an air of relief as two of my managers breathed sighs of relief. "And, by the way, all the money I picked up from the floor of the CEO's office is in an envelope in the top drawer at the extreme left corner of his office."

"And, if I may ask, where else do you work?"

"At U of L," I said, using the popular acronym for the University of Louisville.

"As a janitor?"

"No."

"What do you do?"

"I do research."

"In what?"

"The eye."

"Are you a doctor?"

"Yes."

Twenty-six eyebrows went up, as if responding to a single switch. The subsequent silence was total and hypnotic. Within, I rejoiced. My only wish was to reach Mike and tell him how we "got even," if I may use his favorite phrase.

The building manager thanked me for my candor and dedication before commending MasterClean management for hiring top and reliable staff. What followed next was a total surprise to all; he conceded that he had no specific complaint with our work. All he wanted to do was to get us to "up our output" as was expected of them as the new management of the building. I could hear my manager breathe another sigh of relief.

That evening after the meeting, I received a call from my area manager, the lady at the office. She wanted to know if we could talk. I had no problems with that though I let her know that my time was limited as I had an experiment I must complete before midnight at U of L. She planned to be brief.

She showed up at my site at about 10:30 p.m. bristling with friendliness. Dressed in a loose-fitting dress, she looked like one out on a date, a far cry from the "corporate monster" I met some weeks previously at the office. It turned out that she loved Africans a lot and used to date a man from Ghana. She was surprised that I was wearing a wedding ring even though she wouldn't mind if I was married—all she wanted was @#$%^&*%$#@—I paid scant attention to all the chatter. I did get her business card with her home phone number on the back. And I did promise to call and come over for a drink. I remembered coming down the elevator feeling like Jonah after he disembarked from the fish's belly. With the cool night air playing tricks with my senses, I sauntered to my car like a drunk as I wondered what actually had transpired. So, what changed? Mike could not be more correct. Education does shield one from some of the vagrancies of society. He needed to know he was right again. I believe it would do his ego a lot of good. He would sleep better this night.

I leaned on my battered car as I weighed all these in my mind. The air around the building seemed damp with bigotry. I turned briefly to look at the darkly-stained glass structure. Was my area manager still there? What did that matter? I turned again, tired. Bending over on my car, I believe I farted. Thinking of that now, that part could have occurred only in my thoughts. But as I drove home, something in me told me I was not being fair. Wasn't it my aim to experience racial discrimination? When did the objective change to become a plebiscite on which group treated me right or wrong? And when did it become proper to convict an entire race, gender, and social class for the perceived crimes of a few? Here was I, a living beneficiary of graduate scholarship from perfect strangers, and I am acting as if it never happened. Here was I, a witness to the fairness of the Booth #13 counselor at the U.S. embassy in Lagos, and I am painting an entire population (blacks, whites, Hispanics, Chinese, Africans, and occasional visitors from outer space) with the same tar brush as is meant for a few misguided. Here was I, a person of great learning, ignoring the friendliness of the immigrations officer, the generosity of the restaurant man, the goodwill of countless professors from both Wayne State University and University of Louisville, the infectious humanity of my friend, Dr. Ball, a wonderful soul by all accounts, and I chose to amplify the real and imaginary malfeasance of a handful of the misled. Where did I learn that a handful of negatives outweighs a basketful of good? Here was I, doing exactly what I set out to discover in others. I hissed at the bigot in me.

By the next day, I reminded Mike of the bigot in all of us. As you might expect, he would not have any of "that shit." In the end, we agreed to disagree, leaving a gash in our friendship. Seven years later, that dent is yet to heal. I never saw my embassy friend again. He, too, needed this message. I hope he reads this and, who knows, be convinced of the evil in him and in many of his tribe.

Unoma N. Azuah

Learning to Walk on Black Ice

I arrived at the JFK airport in New York a few years ago, anxious and full of expectations. This is America, a country with roads paved with gold. If the images from the Hollywood movies I watched in Nigeria served me right, America is "God's own country" —nothing short of "heaven." My friend was ready to receive me at the airport. As soon as the immigrations officers let me cross the line to meet waiting parties, I ran into my friend's arms. She had driven all the way from Cleveland, Ohio. My first observation as we pulled away from the airport on our drive to Cleveland was that everywhere was clean. The grasses were green in a lush manner, greener and fuller than any green I had ever seen. The houses were well lined out: well planned. Quite unlike Lagos with its streets littered with all sorts from floating nylon bags, overflowing gutters, and human excreta to poignant stench from bursting trash boxes, deep pot holes, and rugged scrammed up houses.

When we got to my friend's street in Cleveland, the grasses were even greener, but there was an unsettling kind of quietness that blanketed the whole neighborhood. I asked my friend where everybody was. She said that they were either at home or at work. It was a Monday morning. For some reason, I was expecting to see people walking down the streets or chit-chatting as they walked along the roads. The roads were not only wide and vacant, they were stripped of life.

As soon as we arrived at my friend's house and I stepped out of the car, a frosty gust of wind made me realize that the weather was rather cold. I started shivering and a worried frown settled on my friend's face. "If you're shivering in 73-

degree summer weather, what will you do during winter?" I had no answer, but the chill was very uncomfortable. A few days later, she consulted a doctor about my constant shivering. The doctor recommended iron tablets. It helped immensely.

My next discomfort came from the fact that I didn't like American food. It was either too sweet or too greasy. I resorted to eating a lot of boiled rice with canned tuna fish, fried tomatoes, and onions. Also, the quietness in the four-bedroom house and street where we lived was unsettling. I started missing home, but I could not afford to call because I had no money. My friend had none to spare. The only thing to do was to watch TV. The quietness, idleness and not speaking to anybody nearly drove me insane. All of a sudden, I started missing the Lagos noise, the chatter of friends, the poignant smell, and everything I was so eager to escape in Nigeria. When my friend left for work, my constant companions were her two cats. But one of the cats was pitch black. In Nigeria black cats represent a whole lot more than the possibility of owning them as a pet. They are sacrificial objects that are considered the bearers of bad omens. I avoided the black cat as anyone would avoid a poisonous snake. When the cats realized that I didn't like them, they kept out of my way. So my companions became the rustling leaves of lush summer trees and chirping birds.

In due time, school started. I was eager to meet people and make new friends. Yet, making friends did not come as quickly as I expected. Some of my classmates who seemed interested in knowing more about me and where I come from, had mostly questions about Africa. This was when they were not busy asking me to repeat what I had said. They could not understand my accent. So, I spent a lot of time struggling to pick my words to help them understand my statements. It was draining. Needless to say, helping them pronounce my name in the correct manner was futile. They always ended up telling me how musical it is.

My attempts at trying to make friends ended abruptly one fall day in school. A bunch of my classmates were interested in taking me out for lunch—or so I thought—and getting to know me better. When we sat down, the waitress gave us the menu. Since I found all the items in the menu strange, my friends asked me to try out the chicken wings. In fact, they suggested I try the two types of chicken wings—the honey barbecued ones and the hot spicy ones. My mouth watered as they nudged me to place my order. I ordered both types of chicken. I didn't like the sweet-tasting chicken. Sugar had no business with food, I thought to myself. But the spicy hot one I really liked. I ate to my heart's satisfaction, and also asked for a large cup of Coke. It began to feel like America after all—lots of food, big cup of Coke, merriment, rich Americans, chatty friends, etc. I was still brushing off the last bit of my chicken wings when my classmates announced that they were ready to leave. Surprised, I asked them about paying for my lunch. They told me that I had to pay for myself. I was distraught. I asked them to lend me some money to pay. But they said they had exhausted their cash. I asked them to wait for me while I ran across the street to get some money from a friend. They refused to wait. They suggested that if I had a quarter, I could call the friend on the pay phone close to the chair where I sat. I struggled to pull out all the coins in my pocket. I tossed them on the table. I had no idea which one of them was a quarter. They picked out a quarter for me, and I made the frantic call to my friend. She came to my rescue but warned me not to go out to lunch with anybody if I didn't have enough money. I tried to explain to her that in Nigeria when people ask you out for lunch that they usually paid for the meal. She promptly brushed me off, reminding me that this is America and not Nigeria. She also informed me that I had to pay her money back. I did learn, especially with that set of American friends.

As winter came, I was fortunate that my friend was dropping me off at school. After a few weeks though, her job schedule changed. She showed me where and how to ride the train to downtown Cleveland from where I picked a bus to my school. Catching a train was easy; it was climbing an escalator in downtown Cleveland that scared me. I kept telling my friend that I wanted the escalator to stop before I could step in. She tugged at me to put one leg in the escalator and stand on the first step as it moved. I continuously refused, and opted to take the fifty-some flight of stairs instead of the escalator. She then suggested that I should hold onto her while she stepped onto the escalator. That worked, but not without stirring the wrath of waiting pedestrians. Some of them cursed under their breath. Others watched us as if we were circus monkeys. My friend smiled through it all.

Yet another aspect of my frightening experiences was during winter storms and blizzards. I had to walk about six miles, plowing through twelve to twenty inches of snow to get to the train station. I found the overwhelming spread of white snow intimidating. It felt like a sea of white water luring me in to swallow me. In some instances, I would run back home to avoid facing the white plains of snow. But I had to choose between daring the snow to get to school and losing my scholarship for not attending classes.

The tedious walk to the train station was not the only problem. I observed that I started falling on particular sides of the sidewalk. Such falls would often leave me sore, aching, and irritable. Even when I avoided spots where I had fallen, it felt like more spots awaited me somewhere else. I continued falling but couldn't tell why, until my friend revealed to me that I had to learn how to walk on black ice. She schooled me on how to put all my weight on specific parts of my shoes to avoid falling. It worked. My typing posed another problem.

As a graduate student in English, part of my assignments then was to give presentations two times a week. The presentations were not as tasking as the typing of the papers since I had neither computer nor typing background. I finger-picked all the letters on my keyboard. It took me days to finish typing these papers. A number of times I lost typed essays because I had pressed the wrong button. I would begin all over again. I retyped as many times as I lost the essays; these were essays produced through nights of hard study and painstaking finger-typing. Unlike Nigeria where street typists would type papers for anybody at cheap rates, typing was nobody's job in America. I had to learn how to type and use the computer by myself. It took me days of sleeping on my school office floor, days of risking being shot or raped on isolated roads at midnight on my way home, more days of bracing snow storms and blizzards with frozen limbs, and even more days of long studies to maintain my "B" and above grades to keep my scholarship and immigration status.

I could say that I have somewhat mastered the acts of walking the American black ice and typing my class work. It was traumatic at the beginning because it was nothing close to what I had expected to see in America. It was challenging enough, nonetheless, to expand my cuisine habits, my intellectual horizon, and my understanding of the world and life. On the tracks of moving and migrating, there is always black ice to face.

Arrivals

I plough through hills of snow

seeking some warmth in howling winds and storms;

none comes.

I sit before a fireplace

eager to drop ashes in its dying flame...

It's a big house—empty

and the silence threatens to suffocate me.

But winter passes to a lush of green, well-mowed lawns,

blossoming flowers, frolicking butterflies,

the streets are vacant...steam rises from graveyards,

voices recede in narrow hallways

and a white lady, like an apparition, shuffles by with a
      black dog.

We pass

leaning on walls of silence;

the walls trail the tracks of a red train

clattering into the horizon.

The red line runs across my chest;

the green line runs around the rings of my neck.

Life is a train conveying me to bumps of destinies;

the rail lines run across Lagos, Frankfurt, New York, here
    and there

wherever the train heads

and

heaven does not live here.

Crabtree Meadow

Mother, if you were here with me

We could live in the Crabtree meadow

Where there's a forest of firewood

Waiting to cook the meals of many

The trees are dry and ready

Some stand tall but dry and waiting

Some drop their branches like hot spoons

And let them recline—reaching for passersby

Some are gathered like weeds

Waiting to be burnt

Mother, if you lived here with me

We could hunt for crabs in

The Crabtree meadows

and I wouldn't have to wander far to fetch you firewood

But there would be no drums

And no procession of dancers.

In Us

She arrived from the corners of a metal door

hard and bleeding…

She has many maps on her mind, maps that lead to falling
   edges

edges frail like the ache on her back

frail like the frown cracking into roads and boundaries

Boundaries and Barricades

She can't tell a hedge from a fence

But she re-arranges boundaries for when they

become encroaching walls

to lines, so thin, they blur under the sun

She is a woman, old with lines, burdened by boundaries

She is a woman sitting in the corner of a loud life

And she gathers her rags like she gathers her fears

in the face of a gathering storm.

A Tale Out of Ohio

Downtown Cleveland was an open field for our imagination—
a huge tree festered with nests—a sky-tipped tower of market
squares—a buzz of people in multi-colors hurrying away in
different directions—a bunch of junkies staggering around hot
dog vendors and number six buses swerving their way through
curves. We dined often on subways— burger—cheese and
more olives—done, we scuttled along long corridors gazing at
house-sized televisions. Hours were spent darting in and out
of banana republics—the designer stores the rich patronize.
Body and bath had soaps we could only inhale—for most we
scurried in and out. When tired we stood around the square
watching the antics of the American homeless. Sometimes
our gazes settled on a bunch of Christian evangelists blaring
about the end of the world, while pigeons flapped away in
fright. At times we looked at statues of gargoyles spewing
torrid water, and the endless showers of high fountains. In the
belly of these fountains were glittering coins—coins that could
feed us for weeks. A dive and a splash could make us richer,
but a policeman hovers over us like the giant televisions.
We merely stared like a group of starving school kids
gawking at a roasted chicken secured in a glass case.

Downtown Cleveland was the heartbeat of the city, and
we tried to live through its strange rhythm—but it was a world
we couldn't understand or easily adapt to—it was lively,
energized, yet empty and lonely—it was a world so cruel and
cold like the Ohio winter. But we huddled into ourselves—the
two aliens.

Alien

If I were a captive

trapped in the lace of my skin

I would break away like the crust of a caterpillar

and fly like a butterfly.

But I am a captive trapped in the minds of a race

—a swinging rope in the circus of circumstances.

If I were a captive trapped in the lace of my skin

I would break away like the sprouting of a seed

and dwell in a new world.

But I am trapped in the claws of a beast

ravishing the world from the cold.

The winds fool me

I break away from the crowd

set on a trail to trace hoarded treasures.

But my legs scurrying like a spider's

anticipating a crush from the master's boot.

If I were a captive in the race of my skin

I would bleach my life white and strut like a peacock.

But I am trapped in the minds of a race

Unoma N. Azuah

Tropical Storm

It starts with the wind—

a storm wind—

papers, nylon bags, pieces of torn cloths float in the wind,

celebrating before us—

Then falling like tiny pebbles on our metal roofs,

the sound increased to a pounding patter—

like the beats of reluctant drums—

Naked with bare feet

we tear into a run, into the open spaces

as wide as can contain our joy—

we scream, holler, screech, and jump

for the drops licking our skins.

Then it pours, it pours like a burst dam,

It pours, it pours like crashes of waterfalls

And it pours, it pours like yesterday was gone too soon.

Hollering, screaming, screeching, and dancing

in the pull of a hustling rain, sand and mud—

We pour with it

like our lungs would burst through the dams of our chest—

And then it pours, it pours like buckets of water emptying
on us—

But the sky darkens—

Lightning lights up the sky—

Thunder roars—

And our mothers yell their summons—

Azubuike, Okwudili, Ugonna, Unoma, Ejima!

The thunder has stolen our lights.

Like drenched chickens, we waddle in.

It's all memories now

memories as a drop runs down my lip

A rain drop, a tear drop

for scattered images of childhood

Unoma N. Azuah

a rain drop, a tear drop

for a homeland so distant

I grope for the outlines.

Akuba (Grace Quansah)

Victoria Forever Lives

Victoria Adjo Climbié,

Born on All Souls Day

That was November 2nd 1991,

When your short life earnestly began

In Abobo, Ivory Coast,

Where you would grow,

Safe in the knowledge

That you were surrounded

By grounded family and friends who

Truly cherished you,

For the beautiful, bright, and bubbly

Little girl that you were, for all who knew.

We learn that red was your favorite color

And you smiled like a blossoming flower.

Your mother says you were just unique,

So full of kindness and intelligent speech,

The apple of your father's eye,

Yes, you gave your family tremendous pride.

At school, always top of the grade,

What an impact you certainly made

On your elders and class peers,

So much so, that on your return home,

You appeared with a posse of friends

Whom you entertained,

For they loved you to no end.

Then one fateful day,

An aunt took you far away,

With promises of a Western education,

Capitalizing on your parents' humble disposition,

Little did Africa know,

You would never return a lively soul.

The unimaginable abuse you suffered

At the hands of those who claimed to care,

And the incomprehensible professional failures

Of those who were continuously made aware

Akuba (Grace Quansah)

Should never be forgotten,

Yet your life shortened,

Has left us, evermore determined

That your legacy continues to exist,

And even though you are deeply missed

By your parents, siblings, and wider kin

We pledge to ensure your memory forever lives.

114

Tolu Ogunlesi

Paris

You look at one another with

measured smiles, pursed lips,

or absolute hesitations

and speak with your eyes

above the din of your skins

in conversations of many frequencies.

there's the disappointment

that comes when French falls

through the teeth of a kinsman

and you think—

another nigger down.

And there's the Enlightenment

of discovering

that not every black man is

from the country

you left behind.

You glance at one another

in rituals of Suspicion

wondering who's legal

and who smells

of impending deportation.

Paris is the City

where you speak the slowest,

like a stammerer,

to avoid tangling your tongue.

the City where

you find your way

around the fastest

despite their speaking

in tongues.

Out of Gilded Menus

African tourists all, sitting

At The Quay, filling our mouths

With words as we await the white man's food,

Stiff and flattened between the pepper-less pages

Of a carte du jour.

"I'll be darned if Antwerp's bland sauces

Haven't wriggled their way

Into the dishes of Ilfracombe."

"The first culinary commandment of Europe,

For a first time African visitor is this:

Nothing ever tastes as it looks!"

"Every helping of white food tastes

Like it was shaven clean. A distant world

From the spiced afro of African cuisine."

We shall find no rest here –

Not in these bits that sit glumly

On monogrammed plates.

We will eat,

But it is the memories that will silence

Our rumbling stomachs –

Of Lagos, our Lagos, where Isi-Ewu* nightly sails

On raging streams of fresh beer, tongue-paddled,

Headed for the deep oceans,

From whose depths proverbs and Tales by Moonlight

Rise like the mirthful spirits of distant ancestors.

Throughout the days we have left

On this English soil, our backs shall be turned

To all Palaces of Prandial Pleasures. Our plates

Will have no appetites for food out of gilded menus.

We will content ourselves with the smoke that rises

From Lagos' open-air kitchens,

*Isi-Ewu: Goat-head pepper-soup (A Nigerian delicacy)

Tolu Ogunlesi

Smoke that doesn't require a visa to visit us here,

Laden with news of Home and Happenings;

Smoke that darkens the visions

Of sleepy African gods

And the sleepless tempers

Of Europe's Green Garrison.

Coins
(For London)

*Every beautiful city is alike, but ugly cities exist after their own
distinct fashions.*

— The Golden Rule of Travel

You finally absorb that lesson

when with your own eyes you see

that Peckham's really some kind of sewage

dripping quite proudly into the Thames

and that it's true your brothers' muscles

keep Europe's *dusk-to-dawn* wheel a-grinding.

They hide behind oversized newspapers

and under no condition will they invite you

home—because there isn't any.

Or, better still, that council flat

hasn't qualified yet to be upgraded to 'home'.

Tolu Ogunlesi

Much of the time, my dear

you are like one of those machines

that litter London,

that daily digest an eternity

of coins in exchange for every privilege

from a phone call to a pee.

You are just like one of them, gorging

on your own version-of-coins.

Those double-decker buses would be a 5p

and the couples who never hesitate

to lock lips in public

would be a ten.

The neon-irises of those shops

would be a 50p. A drunk, peeing

on a late night sidewalk,

his back to a queue of taxi-drivers

(one of whom is black and looks like

he'd be a Rotarian back home)

would be a one-pound.

A black lady, chubby, careful

not to be familiar with you

as she asks you to raise your feet

so she can sweep beneath,

is a two-pound coin,

because it draws

the biggest response

from your mechanism.

Biggest response, so far.

Many other things would be like notes,

absolutely useless

in a discriminating coin-slot.

Like how the power never fluctuates.

Which is an irony, since it ranked high

Tolu Ogunlesi

on your List

when you stepped

out of Africa.

Now you've grown

used to it, despite

having been here

only forty-eight hours.

Another time, the philosopher in you

would have noted how fast we adapt

and un-adapt

to varied kinds of suffering.

But not now.

The coin-slot is grinding hard,

not sure what kind of currency this would be:

the image of a police car hurtling

downtown, armed with its siren;

side by side with the comment it provokes

from a white man explaining

to a tourist inches from you:

"This is the favorite Bible

passage of the Police here:

Where two or three

blacks are gathered

there we are—

in their midst..."

Small English Towns

The first of them appears in the patch

Of grass between the bottle-bank and the

Paper-bank. (Both banks are stationed

Like armored vehicles at the edge

Of the park—rubbish splayed around them

Like rows of beheaded corpses.) In her arms

Is a bundle of clothes. Clothes, which is odd

Since there are no clothes-banks anywhere

Around town. Another emerges behind

Her. So now they are two-two beads

Of some invisible necklace. And then

The third bead. Male. Stoned like

The others. And just like when you string

Beads, they move closer still, a jamboree

Of joints in an English seaside paradise.

I am beadmaker, fingers apace.

I am god, three floors above;

And black poet, one vain insight ahead.

Terhemba Shija

She Is Nowhere
(For those in diaspora)

The last time I set eyes on my spouse

was four centuries ago when she dived

into the orifice of subterranean waters

And swam to perhaps a distant planet

Since then the rivers have changed their course

And taken new names and darker shades

The hills have folded up and rolled unto Kilimanjaro

and the valleys gathered into the Atlantic

I swam in the belly of the whale

To the Caribbean and the Americas and Canada

and then flew on the wings of the eagle

To Russia and China and the South Pacific

sniffing the grottoes and caverns and catacombs

and prying the medley farms of heaven in vain.

My resonant flute has sung itself hoarse

weary of my bride's incessant praise names

and my ankles have run dry of lubricants

So they screech and howl in pain.

In Jamaica the braided Rasta-man points towards Ababa

taking one step forward two steps backward

to the crazy 'ya reggae rhythm

Uncle Tom sits on the shores of Mississippi

brooding over bloody watermelon and hog meat

Unable to comprehend the fuckin' shit of a

Lost lady

In Moscow the Russians scamper at my songs

Which blow like flames of Chernobyl nuclear holocaust

My thuds have now assumed a regular crashing

trampling the walls of China

and those of Germany

and breaking the underground of London

With a sorcerer's digger

I have excavated the cenotaphs of Europe

And exhumed the dirty ribs of Iago

On the ancient pads of Shakespeare

...And she is nowhere

Neruda wrote the other day

About her shadows fluttering in

The shrines of Obatala in Latin America

And Hughes dreamt he saw a swinging gigolo

Sitting astride her in Harlem

and smiling in thirst for blood

Then at home

At home where my bride set off

The rivers have changed their course

and taken new names and darker shades

The hills have folded up and rolled unto Kilimanjaro

and the valleys gathered into the Atlantic

...But she is nowhere

Diarapha Diallo-Gibert

Têtes de Nègre

"Want some Nigger heads?"

"I'll trade you some Nigger heads for tagada strawberries?"

"Please, Ma'am, how many Nigger heads can I buy for five francs?"

As a child, I was in the bad habit of spending the little money I was given or I had earned on candies in a store that we called, my friends and I, "The lil' grocery." To go there, we had found a route which spared us the trouble of circumambulating the whole neighborhood. We had to go through the garage which was next to the primary school we attended, climb over the portal when it was closed then run across the large Maginot Avenue. The grocer—a tired of living old white woman which was soon to be replaced by her single and world-weary daughter—was seldom if ever amiable to that boisterous group of girlfriends aged six whose warm skin colors and curly or nappy plaited hair revealed the North African or Sub-Saharan origins of at least one of their parents. We always trailed along with us our many even younger brothers and sisters and bothered her several times a day, especially during holiday, for a few cents of multicolored crocodiles, sour jelly French fries, chocolate-covered marshmallow teddy bears and...liquorice Nigger heads. It was twenty-five years ago.

I think I must have been eight years old when, one day, I looked at this black candy flavored with liquorice and commonly called "Nigger head" with new eyes. And, as I was watching attentively to see what I had not yet seen for I had never really observed it before, I discovered the stereotyped visage of a black man in relief: tight curls, bulging eyes, a broad flat nose along with thick lips. Trying to understand the link between the candy and its name – only many years after, in my English linguistics courses, I learned the definition of the sign as a notion and I started to be fascinated by the always arbitrary relation which exists between the signified (concept) and the signifier (the phonological sound) – I understood that what was called a "Nigger head" was that! A vulgar head of a black man which claimed to be the representation of the typical African and accordingly, of my father too. I had never realized that before. I had been blurting out that racist word for years as if it were a shell empty of meaning, for me at least! I had even bought it and worse, I had eaten plenty, more than was sensible. And for a very good reason! It was the cheapest candy ever available, a Nigger, five cents!

Strangely enough, my new perspective made me feel like a cannibal and I was angry against the world and myself as if my own ignorance had played a real dirty trick on me. On the other hand, I also had the feeling that, apart from me, no one seemed to comprehend the serious nature of the situation. For all these reasons, I decided to no longer buy them[1], to give a moral lesson to my brothers and sisters and to refrain from speaking to my friends – be they black, mixed or white – had they refused to follow my example. So, from that moment on, I was regarded as the "rebel on duty" and in the predominantly white environment in which I was growing up and developing my inner self, adults in general and my

---

[1] "The Haribo Nigger head" is now hard to find in stores but one can buy some online. In Belgium, one can still buy "Nigger hands"- shaped chocolates in remembrance of King Leopold II's reign of systematic terror in Congo. For the local people who refused to collect natural rubber or failed to meet the quota imposed by Belgium, a well known practice was to cut off their hands as a type of punishment. This practice was also used to quell the rebellions: soldiers were ordered to bring back the right hands of the rebels they had killed in the forest as an evidence of success and they often cut off the hands of living people, even children, to meet the quota set by their officers.

own white mother in particular were already calling me an "empêcheur de tourner en rond." This strange but accepted French expression literally means "somebody who prevents people from going round in circles" and heaps opprobrium on that person for trying to hinder the smooth running of things in society. As an earthy child, on the contrary, I did not at all grasp how "going round in circles" endlessly and getting nowhere like a flock of sheep lost in a lunatic asylum or embossing liquorice candies with a stereotypical Nigger head in 20th century France could be considered the smooth running of things. Willful as I already was, I decided to take their abuse as a compliment. At the ripe old age of eight then, I made up my mind to wage war on the crass ignorance of the common French citizen and aided by the foolishness of adolescence, I became a bit bolder in my recriminations.

Having developed a very early and vested interest in good cuisine, I tried my gifted hand and sweet tooth at French and international pastry. As such, I took the utmost delight in minutely watching the best pastry chefs and chocolatiers' shop windows everywhere in France and in all the countries I visited abroad in order to learn most of the basic traditional recipes from which I drew my inspiration. What a surprise it was for me to notice that in any good, self-respecting French bakery you could find among the favorite desserts a huge white meringue filled with chocolate butter cream and completely covered with dark minuscule chocolate flakes which bore the sweet name of… "Nigger head."

Undoubtedly, I was cursed! I thus took an interest in this phenomenon in French pastry and discovered, in culinary texts, quite a few racist terms which refer to chocolate desserts such as "tête de nègre" (Nigger head) or "téton de Négresse" (Negress' nipple, so poetic!) and other elaborated puddings that one could not find in a bakery such as the "Négresse" (Negress, a dark chocolate cake with no flour), the "Nègre ou

Négresse en chemise" (Nigger or Negress in shirt, a chocolate mold hedged in a light custard sauce) or the "Nègre blanc" (white Nigger, same recipe except that the mold is coated with whipped cream) and that's not all! I went hunting for my new "Nigger heads" and fomented various offensive strategies: for instance, I would walk into bakeries and ask for a chocolate meringue even though I do not like them. Nine times out of ten, the clerk would stare in surprise before answering to ME, always:

"Oh! You mean a Nigger head?"

When I had the nerve – because believe me, you really need some nerve here—to clearly make the point that I had a preference for "chocolate meringue," at worse she would not even get it, at best she would eventually realize that I was offended. Yet, her answer would always be:

"Come on, there's nothing wrong with that!" or "You shouldn't think the worst of everything, missy!" as if I were the one with a twisted mind.

Let me say that all those people were white, that they did not in the least understand or feel concerned by how much it harmed the Niggers in question or their descendants, whatever the shade of their outer self. Therefore, I stopped buying them and turned to the "praline-flavored meringue," the Métis cousin, coated with lightly toasted crushed almonds.

Five years later, while I was wandering in the streets of my hometown after a long stay in London, I came upon a pastry shop's window in which sat enthroned an astonishing family of meringues. There was an all white "coco ball" coated with grated coconut, a "praline ball," our renowned "Nigger head" as well as a gigantic meringue deep soaked in dark chocolate. Its bulging eyes were made of white chocolate and to draw its disproportionate mouth, the pastry chef had used bright pink almond paste. This disconcerting innovation was called "NEGRO"! I could not believe my eyes. I walked past the window, stopped and as I retraced my steps, I was overcome with pain. Petrified, I stood stock-still there in the middle of the sidewalk, staring at him bewildered. I had the strange feeling that had I decided to go my way, I was cowardly abandoning him to his unfortunate fate: being eaten by white people...cannibals! I walked into the pastry shop with determination although I did not know what I was going to say. Before the clerk had a chance to ask me what I wanted, I uttered:

"Hi, I'd like...uh...uh...'a white man's head'!" Words had come out like that, yet I could have said "a WHITEY"!

She looked at me flabbergasted as if she had just been struck by lightning, as if I had just asked her to give me her own head on a plate and pallid. She stammered: "Uh...uh...uh...I'm sorry but we don't sell that."

"I beg your pardon?" I answered, trying my best to keep calm. "Look at your own window!" And pointing the finger at the meringues, I started to spell out: "Negro, Nigger head, white man's head, easy as pie, don't you think?"

"Oh!" She replied, relieved as she identified the incriminated pastry. "You mean a coconut ball!"

"No, no, you've most certainly misunderstood, I mean 'a white man's head.'" I could have tried to argue the point further but I felt I had made quite an impression on her and that she had almost come within a hair's breadth of a heart attack. Most of all, I realized that it would serve no purpose since she already seemed to be badly infected by the dreadful virus called "denial" that has been rampant in France for a very long time now. She was obviously incapable of connecting the most probably unique experience of being asked for her head to the innumerable subtle humiliations and harassments any so-called "colored" person has to suffer on a daily basis, in our own flesh sometimes. The empathy I expected and wished from her seemed so beyond her understanding of things that I decided it was then time for me to take leave and carry on in my own sweet way. After all, I had lived without it until then and obviously I was going to have to continue to do so. I took my box and went back home where I indulged myself in a little solitary pleasure by savoring my "white man's head" and my victory!

This year, for Thanksgiving, I decided not to stay in Virginia where I teach French at UVA and do research for my PhD in African American history but to go back to France and cover what the mainstream newspapers and body politic called the immigrant "riots." Other, less hegemonic voices preferred to describe the turmoil as a "rebellion" of the French youth of African descent in ghettos surrounding major cities. I could not sit still. I wanted to participate in some way or another in what I had been waiting for and contributing to for more than ten years: a sudden burst, a reveille, the spark which would ignite the fuse of a social revolution. After all, is it not a real French feeling to be in the mood for revolution? How ironic for that new French revolution to come from the most socially disenfranchised and less organized stratum of the "French" population[2] when we are looked down upon as immigrants! I spent a week helping the last resisting forces of my town organize in support of the rebellion and the hundreds of young male rebels imprisoned after immediate trials by an expeditious and vindictive justice supposed to restore law and order. The evening before the demonstration, I was invited to my junior high school friends', Mohamed and Anita, for dinner. It would seem that after four months spent in the USA, I have already Americanized a little since, instead of baking the dessert

---

[2] It seems that things are changing: the CRAN which means courage/ pluck (Representative Committee of Black Associations) was created on November 26, 2005 and aims at becoming "the official interlocutor with the institutions and the Establishment".

myself as I am used to doing on such occasions, I decided to stop by a pastry shop on my way to their house. It was late in the evening and, by some curious coincidence, the only place still open was the big bakery on the same Maginot Avenue where the "lil'grocery" of my childhood once stood.

As I was patiently waiting my turn while the only other client – a white man in his fifties – was being served, almost instinctively my educated gaze began to wander along the refrigerated windows in quest of new techniques and surprising mixings of textures or colors. Of course, I could not help but look for my "Nigger head" and I observed, with joy this time, that things were moving in the right direction, mine anyway. Indeed, I had noticed that the "Nigger heads" had been rechristened "chocolate meringues" in several yet not all French bakeries.

I then recalled that the first time I had noticed this change, in Paris I think, I had resolved to go into all the bakeries which had done the same and engage in a conversation with them. I wanted to congratulate them for their decision to evolve a little and to tell them how humiliating this appellation had been for us. I was glad that this relic of colonialism was gradually disappearing; as far as culinary matters were concerned, at least![3]

---

[3] Here I make reference to the 4th article of the February 23, 2005 Act demanding that school curricula and therefore history teachers acknowledge and teach "the positive role" (sic) of French colonization. It is obvious that this 2005 Act is a response to the May 21, 2001 Taubira-Delanon Act which acknowledged and declared that the transatlantic slave trade and slavery were crimes against humanity and wished that the school history books, at last, dealt with those "dark moments" of French History. A Committee for the Memory of Slavery composed of scholars, historians and associations members chaired by the Guadaloupean writer Maryse Condé was subsequently created and worked on the rewriting of school curricula and history books in particular. They are still waiting for the government to answer and endorse their report submitted in April 2005 to carry out its propositions.

I had never done it before but when the man left and I found myself alone in front of the baker's wife and her employee who were quite amiable despite their long day of labor, I knew it would be that night. After ordering what I had come for and while the baker's wife was packing my cake box, I took the plunge:

"I can see that you no longer name that pastry 'Nigger heads' and, to me it's a really good thing."

"Indeed, it's been a few months since I changed the name," she answered.

"Personally, I thought it was very humiliating for African people and their children born in France like me," I put forward.

"You know, in all the training books, that's the way it was said 'Nigger head' and in bakery schools, it was the way our teachers taught us. We never really paid attention."

Thinking that the change might have been the result of a collective decision emanating from a fraternal order of pastry chefs which now sought to protect the integrity of people of foreign descent against racialist culinary drifts, I ventured:

"May I ask what made you change the name?"

"Yes, of course, to tell you the truth, I had never thought of it before listening to a radio broadcast one day and I remember very well coming down to the closed shop that night, right after listening, to change the name on the label in the window...."

She scarcely had the time to finish her sentence when the man she had just served before me came back in the bakery and, careless of my presence, exclaimed:

"Ah! I forgot my Nigger head. I couldn't go back home without it! May I have one, please?"

Disgusted, I turned away from him to look at the woman's response. A long and icy shiver ran through my spine, my heart sped up, and I could feel feverish pounding up to my temples. All of a sudden, my face began to redden with emotion and anger revealing my also white descent, as it is ironically the case each time I acutely feel that my black heritage is being attacked. So! Changing the name did not help much: a Nigger head was still a Nigger head and for a long time to come! I slipped off my scarf to better breathe and to touch my neck. This time, I was the one who felt as if somebody had just asked for my head! I was bitterly disappointed as if all my little daily struggles were useless in the face of naked ignorance. I felt like asking him whether one single day of his miserable life he had been to school and had learnt how to read a label, I wanted him to look at me in the eyes while uttering "Nigger head," and at the very last moment, the term would die in his throat because I existed, because I was there, standing in front of him... I felt like crying. After our conversation, what could be the owner's reply? I was longing for her to say, in an act of humanity not necessarily motivated by my presence:

"Sorry, sir, but I really don't see what you're talking about. We don't—or I should say we—no longer eat that kind of bread in our shop![4] But, if you prefer, I can give you a delicious chocolate meringue!"

Stopping dead in her tracks, she left my box and, turning to the man, she conceded:

"Sure, let me prepare it for you right now."

---

[4] The French expression "not to eat that kind of bread" means "not to be that sort of person" when you refuse to be involved in something you strongly disapprove of for moral reasons.

Vamba Sherif

The Kingdom of Sebah

"In the beginning, there was a woman." That is how Sebah would tell her version of the story of creation. With these words my mother would bring about much more than she could have guessed.

In our first year in that country there was a lot of snow, and at night a profound silence fell over our neighborhood. One evening I slipped out of bed, tiptoed down the stairs and pushed the curtains at the big window aside a little to look at the yellow-lit houses opposite. Now and then a car would spray up blackened snow. The neighborhood was built in a square, with a playground where no child played, and was screened off from the main street by a large block of flats. The red brick houses were all equally small, as though the inhabitants had a strange concept of space. The big windows downstairs were the same as those on the upper floors, and the blue or brown front doors and even the cobblestone garden paths leading to the houses were all identical. The front and back gardens, tiny patches of ground, were enthusiastically maintained by the inhabitants, and distinguished themselves by the choice of flowers and plants.

The house the four of us occupied was different. The number of the house was barely legible, the paving tiles overgrown with hardy weeds trying to survive that severe winter, and the thick, milk-white curtains of the downstairs windows often closed, so that curious passersby would wonder what was going on behind them. At first, I felt disappointed about my room, which looked out onto the back gardens of the next street, but I slowly got used to it and to the green wallpaper and the poster with clogs on it above the table that my books lay on. Sebah, my mother, had placed my clothes in little piles in the cupboard and asked me to put my dirty laundry into the basket that stood in my room next to my shoes and sandals. The only print on the wall of our living room was a framed poster of the Kaaba in Mecca. Every trace of the previous tenants had been removed. My father had taken the flowering plants away. "They belong outside in the sun, where people can admire them, Sebah," he said. He had given the walls a fresh coat of orange paint, taken down the prints that decorated the kitchen walls, and had thrown them in the bin, followed by a list of local restaurants. A bunch of dried flowers, some doggy posters, and a set of naughty playing cards were removed from the lavatory, leaving its walls bare except for a number of tiles bearing maxims. And there was a glossy picture of the newly elected president on the cover. My bed had gone cold that evening while I was downstairs, but I crawled back in anyway and rolled myself up, close against the radiator, which my father – as fed up with the cold as we were – had turned up full.

My sister Mariam slept in the little attic room and I could hear her tossing in bed. My father had insisted that Mariam and I should each have our own room, for he thought we were old enough to be aware of the differences between us. Sebah, who initially also wanted a room of her own, just as in our home country, had eventually agreed to share a room with her spouse after he won the argument by quoting a learned man with a flawless reputation. Sebah didn't want to talk about it any more, but her husband wouldn't let it rest until he had convinced her, in an open discussion in front of an audience that consisted of their two children. Mariam was seven, two years younger than I, and you could already see what a beauty she was going to be. My sister had my mother's blue-black skin and my father's dreamy eyes. Her luxurious hair, usually in simple plaits, framed a little face, flawless apart from a tiny scar at the side of her nose as a result of constant picking, for she loved dried snot. In character, too, my sister resembled the rest of the family – she was stubborn and often had us speechless.

One morning during that first winter, my father came downstairs to have a cup of tea and he saw Mariam playing outside, dressed in only a thin frock. She was scooping up handfuls of snow, letting it slide through her fingers. She danced, skipped, followed her own footprints, and rolled in the snow. Spellbound, my father watched her, until his parental instincts took over and he called her. But Mariam just carried on with her game. "Sebah, see to it that your daughter behaves herself. We're foreigners here!" my father called out angrily.

Faces

I am one of the thousands who populate the station every morning doing the same thing: boarding a comfortable bus or an air-conditioned express train, or a metro to spend hours seated or moving about doing the same thing. Yet I am different in many ways from those multitudes. My fascination with human faces, oval, elongated, flabby, mustachioed, wrinkled, tender, strong, weak, pale, white, black, brown, yellow, strikes me as perhaps unique. Most mornings, before my transport arrives, a line eleven with an absurd name succeeding the number and that heads for the industrial section of the city, I lean against one of the graffiti walls of the station and watch people stroll by. I see the disappointed face of a woman who'd missed her bus, or the elation of a man who knows he'd arrived half an hour before his transport and can, therefore, relish a breakfast of sausage roll and a cup of black coffee. I cannot help but feel a rush of joy at comparing and contrasting the faces. The face of this one standing beside me, dressed in a suit, is bustling with joy. And that one, sipping at a tea in the station restaurant, has had a good night's sleep, perhaps in the arms of a lover, or she had had a good meal or a pleasant conversation she hadn't had in weeks. That young woman wearing a tense look is perhaps heading for a job interview upon which her whole future depends. A middle-aged man with a vacant stare keeps mumbling something to himself. I go on like this until the board indicates the arrival of my transport and I actually see it pulling to a halt, ready to take me to work.

Occasionally, I acquaint myself with the bearers of those faces. "Excuse me, sir, madam, can you tell me the way to the library?" I would begin. Or I would opt for this line of questioning: "Are you from around here? Yes? Tell me then where to find a good hotel." Or, "The weather looks promising today, doesn't it." Yet still, "I've just moved to this city and don't know the way to the market." These inquiries lead to others. It surprises me how readily I strike up conversation with my acquaintances. To make them believe me, I never hesitate even for a second at revealing an intimate story to the first person I encounter. I tell them about my childhood years and about my mother and father when necessary, especially when I'm talking to a young woman with a chubby face that easily breaks into a sob. I am an expert at chaffing out those types of faces from a multitude: the eyes often sad, the cheeks youngish and red. The gazes are uncertain, afraid of encountering hardness in another face, afraid of being rebuked, thrashed or beaten. I know them when I see them.

"I did not remember my father or meet him until I was sixteen," I would tell a young woman with such a face. "My mother brought me up alone. Many years earlier, she'd faced her parents with the announcement that she was old enough to take care of herself and had left her native island, somewhere in the Caribbean, a twenty-one year old, with hope and a small baggage as her only possession, to carve out a life for herself in Europe. Confronted with harsh weather that threatened to eat her bones away, my mother had struggled on. Before thirty, she'd completed her studies and had landed a job at an insurance company. Then she had met my father. It was love at first sight. Or perhaps my mother was charmed by the storytelling gift of the man. My father would fabricate stories that spanned centuries, taking off from Europe and ending up at his birthplace: a small town in Brazil whose population spoke Yoruba, one of thousands of languages spoken in Africa. The stories would encompass America, crossing over to Africa, to an obscure village which he would pinpoint on the African map. My mother was head over heels in love with his positive outlook at things, which, as she later discovered, made him less ambitious, taking things as they came. My father shied away from a marriage in which he had to have a say. He never wanted to have a say in anything. My mother rose in the ranks of the society and towered above her husband in everything. And she took me with her. I attended some of the best schools, spoke the standard Dutch, English, German, and Spanish fluently, and I befriended the privileged. Meanwhile, my father, a player at the periphery of things, a dreamer who took orders from his wife, cooked for her, ironed her clothes, and brought me to school, sleeping with his eyes wide open and dreaming and hoping of being as successful as his wife, suddenly realized one sleepless night, that there was no village in Africa with such a ridiculous name, and that taken by a desire to know his past, he'd romanticized Africa and had ended up believing it himself. So tortured was my father with this discovery and the fact that it'd taken him so long to get to it, that he rose from bed one night and slipped out, taking along a family portrait. When she discovered that he'd gone, my mother never shed a drop of tears or ever mentioned his name in our home again. She went on to become a successful businesswoman with a company of her own.

Many years later, sixteen to be precise, a bald old man, stooped under the weight of years and bitter experience, stood ringing the doorbell of our new home. When I opened it, I could not place the jaundiced face that stared at me. The old man shoved me aside and started for the kitchen to fetch a drink. I wanted to scream at him, but his stolid manner checked me.

"Don't stand there gaping at me," he roared. "Have you no manners! Or is it because all your mother does is spends her time gathering wealth and has no time for you."

It was then that it dawned on me that I was gaping at the storyteller whose craft had eventually smothered every real ambition he ever had. The old man looked wretched and reeked of the smell of a month's garbage. He spoke in snatches and hisses as though angry with the world. In those few hours, he ordered me around, lorded it over me, telling me how to behave in the presence of a guest.

I sat there oppressed by his presence, but unable to wrench myself away from the yoke of the power he exercised over me. I had hoped for a father, had even imagined him, whenever we talked about our fathers at school as being perfect, as being the accumulation of all the things admired: handsome, cultured, educated, smartly dressed like I had always wanted to dress when I became an adult and had a job of my own. But the angry old man was different and was not doing his best to conceal it. He hammered into my ears the responsibility of a son to the father and mother and to himself. Unprepared, I was now confronted with a man who preached the very credo of life to me.

That evening my mother came home. She looked strikingly beautiful, a sharp contrast to that emaciated person that was my father. I was horrified to see her fling her slender arms around him. "But why, mother?" I cried. My sudden outburst took the two by surprise.

My father sucked his teeth and ran toward me, perhaps intending to slap or reprimand me, but my mother beat him to me. She cupped my head in her hands and said simply: "Because he makes me laugh."

I left them and went upstairs to my room and buried my head under a pillow. Later, I heard my father come in. He sat on the bed and began one of his stories. He told the story of a man who, to please his ever demanding wife, left his village in search of a river that changed a white cloth into black. The man traveled for years until he came to a town with the magic river. There and then he decided, upon testing the power of the river, never to return to his wife.

We sat in silence for a while, and perhaps in that silence he expected me to say something, a word that could break the wall he'd built between us. But I couldn't. Finally, he left the room but not before ruffling my head. I heard the two talking downstairs.

When he was about to leave, my mother escorted him to the door and planted a kiss on lips and she returned, sobbing before my very eyes. "I still love him," she said.

"That's what love does to people," I would tell a young woman wearing a beautiful shawl, who keeps fingering her blonde hair. She wears an anxious look. Now and then she would divert her attention from me to the boards to see whether her bus had arrived. "I never saw my father again," I would continue my story. "The last time we heard about him was that he'd settled in an American city and was teaching its inhabitants African history, traditions, and customs, reminding them of their origin. He even convinced some of them to take a pilgrimage to the land of the ancestors. Now, after many years, my father is a professor of African studies at a prestigious university."

"I continued to live at home with my mother. But at a certain moment in life, some years after my father's visit and my graduation as an architect, and when everything I did suddenly appeared to me as the work of a responsible and matured young man, I decided to move to a place of my own. I had met a girl."

"Never before had I experienced such bliss as in the company of that girl. I saw my future as inseparable from hers. She was a true lover, who understood my silences, my mumbles, my unfinished phrases. Many times, we would spend the day together quenching the yearning we'd built up for each other the day before. And when she left to go home, it was as if we were parting for the last time. After a love affair of two years, three months, two weeks, a day, and two hours of sheer bliss, she took my love away to a sunshine island. On getting there, she sent me a greeting card telling me that my love was with her, lodged deep in her breast, nurtured every day."

"I met her at one of the annual festivities jointly hosted by the Antilleans and Surinamese community. She struck me as so delicate that I chose my words carefully when talking with her. Even when I won her, which took more than a year to achieve, I had to wait for a week to muster enough courage to be intimate with her. It was a summer night when it happened, the air peppered with the fragrance of flowers of midsummer. I counted the stars of the heavens as I soared toward them, and I sobbed as everything about me bore the effulgent colors of bliss. Just beholding her, those eyes, those pert breasts, sometimes numbed me with a fervent desire."

At this point my beautiful audience would begin to gape at me, to imagine the woman I had described, to imagine herself being that woman, which had been my plan all along. Before boarding her bus, she would ask me to meet her at a cafe or a discotheque, and I would see the longing to be loved and kissed by those lips which had told such a wonderful story. I would never show up.

Not long after the girl would leave, I would strike up conversation with a well-dressed young man in a colorful tie who works multinationally. I would tell him that what I found beautiful about the city are definitely its people. A faint smile would light up his face. I would know then that I had entangled him in my web of influence. That in a few minutes he would tell me that he's been promoted to a manager and is engaged to a girl. That very much I am sure of.

I take up the thread of my narrative about my first love and the letter I had received from her. "I remember her chuckles," I would tell the young man. "One can never tell what lies beneath a chuckling voice until it blurts out with a word. Then you tremble and surrender and suffer and love. The letter was vague. It never mentioned love; it beat around it, like one does around a dish you loathe and have sworn never to eat. I knew then that my love had been thrown to the air of that beautiful, sun-scorched island, that it had been buried somewhere deep down in its sand, that it had fallen and had been kicked around, that rain had wet it, that fever had caught it and it had trembled, hanging upon its last breath, remembering a vague face that was mine.' "Shocked by the letter," I would tell my listener, "I had gone mute." I would demonstrate it. "My period of muteness lasted for days. Only then did I come to terms with the fact that a woman had stolen my love and while the love was still alive, she'd dressed it up in palm-fronds—the symbol of death—and she'd watched it choke to death."

I would leave the floor open for my young audience, the newly appointed manager, and he would play the seasoned actor. He would say things he'd never told even his mother. I would lead the string of the play, swearing when need be, smiling or laughing. My acquaintance would depart contented. I would promise myself to remember the expression on that face that day and compare it with the one I would see a week, months, or even a year after.

Often after work, I would feed my tomcat Ramses. It would climb upon my lap and lick at its paws, staring intently at me as though it wanted me to share my daily experience with it. Sometimes I would tell it an entire story while ruffling its head. Then I would sit before a dinner of canned or fast food, mostly Chinese. Thereafter I would remember the faces I had seen that day and would categorize them: the striking in one group, the pretty in another, or the ones that fell in between the two in another group, and ones that were not beautiful in yet another. I would search for a feature in the non-beautiful ones that attracted me: the shape of the nose, the lashes or the brows, the lips or the ears, and hair style. If I thought they were not enough, I would concentrate on the body contours, on the legs, the arms, the shoulders, the neck, and so on. I would draw the features never employing color but a pencil. I would work until one in the morning, sleep for six hours, and then rise to prepare for work.

I take my work at the architectural firm very seriously though I detest the routine of doing the same thing day after day. That's why, during my first year of working there, I developed means and ways of doing things differently but efficiently. I was to later discover that it worked to my advantage. My boss, the firm owner, Mr. Klein, was impressed and we became friends.

He often invited me for dinner at his sprawling villa tucked away somewhere outside of the city, to the amusement of his family: Mrs. Klein, a silent wife who muffles her laughs as I tell my many anecdotes and jokes; Astrid, a voluptuous daughter with auburn hair who steals glances at me; and Mark, a boy of ten, who never tires of asking me to tell him stories. Most of the time I would contrive an excuse. But when I did tell him a story and suddenly remember my father, I would stop. I had sworn never to take after a storyteller less I be damned by the craft. Mark would urge me on. But the moving face of my father surrounded by a group of people stares out at me from the wall and I would shake my head.

Dinner would be succeeded by delicious desserts. Then Mr. Klein would take me by the arm and lead me to the study. There he would narrate the family history from the advent of the Spaniards, the French, the First and Second World Wars, to the present day. He would show me his family tree, mentioning detailed histories of each family member with an accuracy that would astound me. In pat manner, he would mention the dates of their marriages and death and the relationship each held with the other. It was a diverse family tree, comprised of Spanish, French, English, and German branches. "You are a hard-working young man, Louis. I see the future of my company in you," he would say. We would chat on, while listening to a new age number which he claimed soothed the nerves.

As if it'd been planned, Astrid would intrude on us at this point. Her father would immediately leave us. We would talk about trivial things; I was not in love with her and never wanted to try, and I would leave late at night to spend hours drawing faces, while my only companion, Ramses, sat beside me, never retiring to sleep while I stayed awake. In the morning, I would head for work. At noon, I would spend lunch sometimes at the station, observing people.

On most weekends, I would visit Mom. She would hug me, imploring me to move back to the house.

A year ago, as I hurried to take my bus, I saw an old black woman who was different from the many I encountered every day. Despite her old age, she looked striking and composed. I paid less attention to her because I was in haste. Upon my return at noon, I saw her again, seated on one of the white-washed benches, reading the papers. The next morning I saw her standing erect like a goddess, bold and graceful, looking at the station as though it were her realm and the people her subjects. Something about her stopped me from approaching her. Every day, from then on, I left work with the certainty that I would see the old woman. I often drew her face over and over again.

Today, Saturday, I've decided to meet her. It is dry, but the weather might change, as the skies are clouded. I dress in my best and throw on my summer jacket, get in my car which I make use of only on weekends. Then I drive to the station. When I approach her, she calls me her son and tries to hug me. With the intention of unraveling the mystery she'd become or perhaps taken by the tenderness in her voice, I agree to drive her home. She calls an old white man who talks to me as if I were his son, someone he'd known all his life. The white man tells me about a girl with whom I was once in love: his daughter. He talks about her with such tenderness that tears spring to my eyes.

Then I see her portrait. I stare at the gilt frame painting of a slim, sickly white girl, in a thin, slick dress, her long hair carelessly bundled. She bears a sad but, upon a closer look, very defiant gaze in her eyes. The painter had thrown her amidst a chaos of flames, bullets, ruins, refugees, emaciated bodies, flies, plagues, hunger, and drought. Why the girl? I could not help but wonder, almost aloud. Why portray her like that? What was the artist trying to achieve? I could see that he was drawing war. But why the girl?

When the old man leaves, and the woman goes up to dust a room she says is mine, I decide to leave. But on my way home, I realize that I have wronged her and myself. That I cannot lead a happy life making unhappy someone who'd enriched my life in so short a time. Perhaps, I'll return one day.

References

Arthur, John. (2000). *Invisible Sojourners: African Immigrant Diaspora in the United States.* Westport, CT: Praeger.

Du Bois, W.E.B. (1999). *Souls of Black Folks.* Henry Louis Gates, Jr & Terri Hume Oliver (Eds). New York: W.W. Norton & Company.

Hatton, Timothy. J. & Williamson, Jeffrey G. (2005). *Global Migration and the World Economy.* Cambridge, MA: MIT Press.

Inchbald, Elizabeth. (2007). *A Simple Story.* Anna Lott (Ed). Orchard, New York: Broadview Press.

International Organization for Migration (IOM). (2008). http://www.iom.int

Loucky, J, Armstrong, J & Estrada, L. J. (2006). *Immigration in America Today.* Portsmouth, NH: Greenwood Press.

Migration for Development in Africa: Mobilizing the African Diasporas for the Development of Africa. (2007). International Organization for Migration. http://www.iom.int/jahia/Jahia/cache/offonce/pid/1674?entryId=16306

Postma, Johnannes. (2004). *The Atlantic Slave Trade.* Portsmouth, NH: Greenwood Press.

Shinn, David H. (2002)."Reversing the Brain Drain in Ethiopia." An Address delivered before the Ethiopian North American Health Professionals Association (Alexandria, VA. November 23). http://chora.virtualave. net/brain-drain8.htm. Accessed July 2008.

United Nations Economic Commission for Africa (ECA). (2004). http://www.uneca.org. Accessed October, 2008.

Vesely, Milan. (2005). Africans in the U.S.: Second Wave Migrants Outdo African Americans." *African Business* 309, 38-40.

World Migration 2005: Costs and Benefits. (2005). World Migration Report Series: International Organization for Migration.http://www.iom.nt/jahia/Jahia/cache/offonce/pid/ 1674?entryId=932

World Migration in 2008: Managing Labour Mobility in Evolving Global Economy. (2008). World Migration Report Series: International Organization for Migration. http://www. iom.int/jahia/Jahia/cache/offonce/pid/1674?entryId= 20275

Notes on Contributors

Padmore Enyonam Agbemabiese is a Ghanaian poet, playwright, and scholar currently lecturing at Ohio State University. He received his elementary education in Ghana at Abor Roman Catholic Primary School and later his secondary education at Abor and Kpandu secondary schools. Growing up in Ghana, his grandma never left him uninformed about his cultural identity and heritage. The basic statements of his grandma helped shape his educational views.

Unoma N. Azuah teaches English at Lane College in Jackson, Tennessee. She is an MFA graduate of Virginia Commonwealth University, Richmond, Virginia. She also has an MA in English from Cleveland State University, Cleveland, Ohio. Her undergraduate degree in English is from the University of Nigeria, Nsukka. She has received a number of awards for her writing, which include the Hellman/Hammett award, the Leonard Trawick award, Urban Spectrum award and the Flora Nwapa/Association of Nigerian Authors award. She has published a novel entitled *Sky-High Flames* and a collection of poems, *Night Songs*.

Lisa Day-Lindsey, co-editor of the anthology, is an Assistant Professor of English at Eastern Kentucky University. Her research and teaching interests focus on early and nineteenth-century American literature as well as Caribbean literature. She received her doctoral degree in American and MultiEthnic Literature from Southern Illinois University at Carbondale.

Diarapha Hélène Diallo-Gibert was born in Tours, France, in 1974 and has a double French and Malian nationality/ citizenship. She is a certified English Teacher (CAPES) and earned a DEA degree from the Université de Poitiers. She is a doctoral candidate at the Université de Provence and is working on a dissertation entitled *Full-Blooded State: Anti-Miscegenation Laws and Eugenic Discourses against Social Equality in 1920s Virginia.* Since 1992, as the chairwoman of Just Justice, a French association against the death penalty, she has been involved in the campaign to free journalist Mumia Abu Jamal from Pennsylvania's death row. Her most recent publication includes an article, "Mumia Abu Jamal," in *Encyclopaedia of the African Diaspora: Origins, Experiences, and Culture,* ed. Dr. Carole E. Boyce-Davies, 2008.

Sheikh Kumarr Kamarah is an Associate Professor of English and teaches linguistics, literature, and writing at Virginia State University. He was educated at Fourah Bay College in Sierra Leone, Leeds University in England, and the University of Wisconsin at Madison, USA. He has published two volumes of poetry, a book of grammar, and several articles in refereed journals.

Nicholas Makoha is a poet, teen mentor, and educationalist who has performed internationally. Of Ugandan heritage, he resides in the UK and was a featured artist on Kin, a 45-venue UK tour of writers, DJs, and musicians that explored the theme of kinship in 2003-2004. In 2005 he supported London's bid for the Olympics, Back the Bid, through writing and performing a poem, "The Measure of All Things." For Black History Month, he toured the Czech Republic with the British Council. As a founding member of Malika's Kitchen, he has led workshops in Chicago high schools. His first collection of poetry is entitled *The Lost Collection of an Invisible Man.*

Wadzanai Mhute was born and raised in Zimbabwe. An avid reader with a passion for writing, she currently resides in the United States. Her writing has appeared in *Afrique News Magazine, Mimi Magazine, MethodX, Per Contra,* and *Philadelphia Weekly.*

Suzannah Mirghani is a doctoral candidate in the field of Communication and Media Studies at Eastern Mediterranean University. Currently, she is a part-time Research Assistant in the Center for International and Regional Studies at Georgetown University School of Foreign Service in Qatar. She is Russian-Sudanese, and she writes poetry and short stories and is a freelance translator and editor.

Tinashe Mushakavanhu is a Zimbabwean writer and academic. He holds a degree in English from Midlands State University and a master's degree in Creative Writing from Trinity College, Carmarthen in Wales. His PhD is culminating in a comparative study of Percy Bysshe Shelley and Dambudzo Marechera. He is completing work on a short novel, *The Harare Hermit.*

Rhoda Ndagire Mwanje was born in Kampala, Uganda, and received a degree in literature and education at Makerere University. She has since worked as an editor and received a master's degree in Literature in 2001 from the University of Gothenburg in Sweden. In 2002 she relocated to the USA and is currently studying for a master's degree in Education at George Mason University.

Salome C. Nnoromele, co-editor of the anthology, is the Director of the African/African-American Studies and Professor of English at Eastern Kentucky University. She received her undergraduate degree from the University of Utah. Her master's and doctorate degrees are from the University of Kentucky. She is the author of several books and articles on African culture and literatures. She was born and raised in Nigeria.

Mansim Okafor was born in 1952 in Calabar, Nigeria. He has a master's degree in Biology and a doctoral degree in Human Physiology from Wayne State University. Having published three collections of poetry, *Chinelo, Rainbows on Angel Wings*, and *The Parable of the Lost Shepherd*, his writing focuses on social injustice and religious bigotry. He sees his writing as his only form of outreach to a world that is fast forgetting the art of being human. He is currently an Associate Professor of Physiology at St. Catharine College, St. Catharine, Kentucky, where he lives with his wife, Judith, and their three children.

Tolu Ogunlesi was born in 1982 in Nigeria. He is the author of a collection of poetry, *Listen to the Geckos Singing from a Balcony*, published in 2004.

Akuba (Grace Quansah) is a Ghanaian-descended single mother of four children, particularly committed to empowering black learners to achieve highly in education. She creates her own folktales and enjoys writing poetry, which has been published in anthologies and has received many awards. Her poem "The Awakening of Elmina" is included in *Unheard Voices*, an anthology of slave narratives to commemorate the bicentenary of the abolition of the Trans-Atlantic slave trade. She has also published academic papers and conference reports, and is currently a freelance facilitator at the British Museum.

Vamba Sherif is a Liberian writer residing in the Netherlands. His novels include *Bound to Secrecy, The Kingdom of Sebah,* and *The Land of the Fathers,* all of which were published in Dutch. His first novel, *The Land of the Fathers,* is about the founding of Liberia by free blacks from America.

Terhemba Shija holds a BA in English and Literary Studies from the University of Calabar, Nigeria, a master's degree in Creative Writing from the University of Maiduguri, and a PhD in African Literature from the Benue State University in Nigeria. She currently teaches Critical Theory and African Literature at the Nasarawa State University, Keffi, Nigeria.

Zena Tesfaye-Teferra, a painter and poet, has spent almost half her life away from her country of Ethiopia. She studied Economics in England and International Relations in Northern Virginia, and still finds the idea that she might be thinking in English somewhat hilarious. She is currently back in Ethiopia for at least a year and hopes to find answers, such as what languages she dreams in while in Addis Ababa.